Influence Design in the AI Era

Influence Design in the AI Era

Business Strategy

Sean W. Smith

BEP

BUSINESS EXPERT PRESS

Leader in applied, concise business books

Influence Design in the AI Era: Business Strategy

First published in 2025 by
Business Expert Press, LLC
222 East 46th Street, New York, NY 10017
www.businessexpertpress.com

ISBN-13: 978-1-63742-814-6 (paperback)
ISBN-13: 978-1-63742-815-3 (e-book)

Business Expert Press Collaborative Intelligence Collection

First edition: 2025

10 9 8 7 6 5 4 3 2 1

EU SAFETY REPRESENTATIVE
Mare Nostrum Group B.V.
Mauritskade 21D
1091 GC Amsterdam
The Netherlands
gpsr@mare-nostrum.co.uk

To Jennifer and Macie, my wife and daughter, and my partners in every adventure life throws our way. This book is a testament to our love and a celebration of all we've built and continue to build together.

Description

Finding a balance between humans and intelligent machines has become paramount. While ingenious AI solutions may yield immediate benefits, they can also trigger behavioral shifts, potentially leading to long-term challenges and shifting standards.

Influence Design in the AI Era: Business Strategy **is a must-read for business leaders and strategists seeking to understand and capitalize on AI's transformative power.** Through the lens of influence architecture, organizations can harness AI's capabilities to drive desired outcomes, enhance situational awareness, and gain control in the digital landscape.

The book offers **practical strategies for alignment, fosters collaborative intelligence, and lays the foundation for a "machineforce"**—the organization's harmonious collective of artificially intelligent machines dedicated and aligned in support of organizational productivity.

As a comprehensive guide, **this book empowers the influence architect in us all** to thrive in the AI era and beyond. It forges our path toward the Machineforce Era, in which humans and machines collaborate seamlessly to shape a sustainable future.

Contents

Testimonials

"In the same way, a ship going on a voyage into undiscovered lands needs a navigator, and every organization embarking on a journey to incorporate AI into their business needs an influence architect. In Influence Design, Smith outlines a framework for the practical adoption of AI through real-world examples and case studies to illustrate how organizations can optimize processes, enhance decision-making, and foster innovation.

Like many powerful technologies that came before, successful adoption came from the organizational transformation that occurred in parallel. Smith's Influence Design is a must-read for business leaders, strategists, and technologists who want to understand how AI can enhance business transformation strategies through increased organizational productivity through practical insights."—**Matt Maccaux, Head of AI Customer Engineering, Google Cloud**

"AI's true power lies in its ability to enhance decision-making and shape the future of business. Sean W Smith presents a compelling vision for leveraging AI as a force for influence and innovation. Smith's Influence Design provides an essential toolkit for navigating the intersection of AI, influence, and strategy. It is a crucial read for those looking to create a lasting impact in an AI-driven world."—**Andreas Deptolla, Chief Technology Officer (CTO) at Atari Inc., Co-Founder and Board Member of Thrivepass Inc.**

"In the dynamic landscape of sports and entertainment analytics, 'Influence Design in the AI Era' provides a crucial framework for harnessing the power of AI while preserving the human element in critical decision-making. Smith's insightful exploration of the 'Influence Architect' role, responsible for strategically integrating AI and human expertise, is indispensable for any organization seeking to optimize performance and cultivate sustainable growth. Moreover, the book's in-depth analysis of 'Machineforce,' the driving power of AI, illuminates how to leverage its predictive capabilities ethically and transparently, fostering trust among stakeholders. This book is a must-read

for anyone looking to navigate the complexities of AI in business, ensuring responsible implementation and maximizing its potential for strategic advantage."—**Brian Kelsey, Kraft Analytics Group**

"*Sean Smith has a way with words, taking a complex and vast subject such as AI and breaking it down into understandable pieces that create a foundation for one's learning. This is a must-read to start your educational journey on AI and how to use it for good going forward.*"—**Scott H. Roth, Chief Customer Officer & Advisor to Founders**

"*In a world where artificial intelligence is revolutionizing the business landscape,* Influence Design in the AI Era: Business Strategy *offers essential insights for organizations navigating the future and provides a roadmap for aligning AI-driven strategies with the evolving needs of today's Software-as-a-Service (SaaS) customers. This book empowers businesses to innovate with AI, foster trust, enhance customer relationships, and deliver meaningful, responsible outcomes that drive long-term success.*"—**Andrew Fink, VP of Customer Experience**

Acknowledgments

No words can sufficiently express my gratitude to my family, friends, and colleagues who supported me on this journey.

To my wife and daughter: I'm deeply grateful to my wife, Jennifer, and my daughter, Macie, for their patience and understanding during the long hours and mental focus required to bring this book to life. Thank you for supporting me through the late nights and the inevitable "always-thinking" distractions. Your love and support kept me going. I am thankful for your infinite sacrifices to accommodate my passion in your world. You keep me going by just being there for a chat, supporting my distracted focus, and lifting me when I am in self-doubt. I'm so grateful to have you both in my life!

To friends and family: Thank you for believing in me and what I do. From your questions and examples to your support, the energy you bring, and the motivation you give to keep me going, thank you for the amazing conversations, feedback, and continuous support.

To professional colleagues: Thank you for your collaboration and feedback. Your generosity in sharing your wisdom and knowledge has been essential to our work. I am incredibly grateful for the professional development opportunities and mentorship you have given me over these years, which have transformed my writing and thinking skills.

To my illustrative partner: Adam Sollien, working with you on this project has been a pleasure. Your creative interpretations and stunning visuals have elevated the work beyond my expectations. Thank you, and I look forward to continuing our partnership!

… and to my readers, I sincerely hope this book ignites your imagination and empowers you to build foundations for the machineforce of your dreams.

Thank you all for joining me on this journey!

Introduction

Embracing Evolutionary Optimism and the Rise of the Machineforce

My journey with AI began almost two decades ago, sparked by the potential of superintelligent machines. I envisioned a future where technology and humanity would seamlessly collaborate, fostering an engaged and connected workforce. Though somewhat abstract, my initial vision has been refined over years of research, debate, and innovation into the core concept driving the influence design in the AI era: alignment.

These pages are not just a collection of words; they represent a profound commitment to a new mindset toward symbiotic relationships with intelligent technology. I aim to inspire a transformation in individual and collective thinking, empowering organizations to leverage AI for strategic victories. Over time, my journey has evolved into a deeper understanding of human behavior and the fundamental elements that drive operational success.

True innovation transcends mere replication or enhancement of existing methods. It involves recognizing and appreciating each organization's unique characteristics and guiding them through positive change. Throughout my experience in analytics product companies, service organizations, and public service, I've observed countless attempts to force new technology into old ways of work. The allure of innovation is undeniable, with the latest technologies emerging daily, promising to revolutionize outdated business processes. However, rushing to adopt these solutions without careful alignment can be detrimental.

A common pitfall I've encountered is the relentless focus on identifying a "use case." While well-intentioned, the question often narrows its scope and obscures complex processes and transactions that technology can truly impact. Actual use cases lie in the broader narrative of growth and transformation, an area of interest, not solely in deploying specific technology. It's about balancing human ingenuity and machine intelligence, optimizing costs, fostering adaptability, and achieving profitability beyond market shares.

This series on influence design in the AI era aims to equip leaders and organizations with the knowledge and wisdom to navigate a world where humans and intelligent machines thrive together. By fostering a culture of continuous improvement, leveraging AI for data-driven decision making,, and promoting collaboration, any entity can achieve its goals more effectively.

Ultimately, strategic progress transcends individual goals; it's about working toward a brighter future for everyone. The principles outlined here are not limited to the corporate world; they empower nonprofits, government agencies, and community groups to embrace technology and data for strategic advancement, creating a more inclusive and prosperous future.

With foundational principles established and the vision for a brighter future taking shape, I couldn't be more thrilled to bring this all together. The fusion of human potential and technological advancements holds immense promise, and I'm filled with excitement and anticipation for the journey ahead.

This work lays the foundation for a groundbreaking new discipline: influence architecture. It uniquely expands on governance, compliance, and risk management with the power of influence and behavioral science to optimize an organization's machineforce. At its helm stands the influence architect, a visionary leader who understands the technical intricacies of AI and possesses a deep understanding of human behavior and organizational dynamics. The influence architect acts as a bridge between the human workforce and the machineforce, ensuring seamless integration and maximizing the potential of both. Through this holistic approach, organizations can truly harness the power of AI while fostering a culture of innovation, responsibility, and sustainable growth.

Beyond individual goals or organizational success, it's about creating a world where innovation, collaboration, and ethical considerations guide us toward a more equitable and prosperous future for everyone. The path forward is filled with possibilities.

I'm eager to explore with you, step-by-step, as we navigate the ever-evolving landscape of AI and build foundations for the coming Machineforce Era.

CHAPTER 1

Crafting Tomorrow

The Mastery of Digital Influence

Within an intricate dance of ones and zeros, logic takes shape, quietly orchestrating a symphony of transformations that may or may not be immediately apparent in your daily life. Whether facilitating seamless transactions, fine-tuning the ambiance of your home, or, in critical moments, swiftly applying brakes to avert potential tragedy, binary wizardry collides at the core of machines, shaping the contours of your existence. "Whether we are talking supply chain predictions or finance modeling, vaccine design or manufacturing scale up, data-powered software systems are operating the company."[29] The influence of code extends beyond mere convenience. It now makes critical ethical decisions in milliseconds, impacting lives and blurring the line between human actions and artificial intelligence (AI; Figure 1.1).

Figure 1.1 This fits you right now ...

Influence, A Digital Art?

We now live in a world of code-based influence. Logic running on some machine, somewhere, possibly even in the cloud, has influenced and continues to affect you. Consider, at its simplest, the alarm clock on your nightstand. In the distant past, you plugged it in and configured specific details, such as wake-up time, and it has been influencing you for days, weeks, months, and years. That simple alarm clock has now transformed into a smartwatch capable of intelligently rousing you during your lightest sleep phase, making it much easier to rise from bed. Hyper-tuned to your body rhythm, the intelligent accessory guides you toward optimal wake-up time for a productive day, even when light levels and sleep needs vary. Regardless of ideal situations with machine intelligence, we face a fundamental problem: You're the one who must wake up, but you may not be the one setting the alarm, and well, even more appropriately, in some circumstances, you may not even be aware of it.

The buzz around AI keeps growing louder as groundbreaking technologies change various elements of our lives. It's hard to miss the never-ending deluge of articles, posts, and news stories about magic machines that have or will, at some point, deliver transformational value. A recent McKinsey report, "The State of AI in early 2024," highlights a significant surge in AI adoption, driven partly by the growing interest in generative AI. "After remaining stagnant at around 50 percent for six years, AI adoption has jumped to 72 percent in 2024." More encouraging, "This trend is global, with over two-thirds of respondents across almost all regions reporting AI usage in their organizations. The professional services industry saw the most significant increase in adoption."[1]

Even with growing adoption, the ever-raging fire of AI and its immense unknowns still imperil us as fundamental problems based on statistical complexity. The fearful cast of "machines that learn?!?" creates a feeling of ambiguity and inquisitiveness. Nestled within the whirlwind of excitement and change is the genuine, sometimes forgotten question: what does it mean when machines learn? Amidst all the AI hype comes a constant reminder: AI's technological marvel will be woven into every fiber of our society—from personalized shopping recommendations to predictive maintenance; its supportive role is ever more present to show us what might lie ahead.

As adoption accelerates, it's worth expanding our perspective on AI teams by transforming the image of statistical technicians into extraordinary artists and rethinking how we staff teams and align roles with broader organizational objectives. AI professionals deep in data, statistics, and code can have difficulty thinking instinctively about artistic dimensions. By releasing art's extraordinary power, we can contribute innovative thoughts and a disruptive competitive edge waiting to be unlocked through strategic insight. With enough talent under the proper guidance, AI teams can work as hidden architects of influence who can subtly move opinions and behaviors to foster positive outcomes. As the artistry of subtle interaction design, influence can shape human behavior for a particular purpose without audience awareness. While AI teams will undoubtedly have many uncontroversial applications, ranging from traffic optimization to cookie-click-optimization mechanisms for advertisers everywhere, their true power isn't in top-down control; they are now the best mind navigators and outcome nudgers with more accurate predictive muscle than we poor mortals can ever hope to muster. It's an art form of influential brush strokes that work best when they appear natural, seamlessly enhancing outcomes rather than rearranging any course. AI is just that: a limitless strategy tool—changing the game for organizations and providing the ability to shape the future in ways never previously possible. Focusing heavily on influence over intervention, AI artists can profoundly change the sequence of supportive events by setting up robust opportunities upstream from desired outcomes, especially in different contexts. Achieving artistic mastery of AI beyond automation is a gradual process during which some organizations flourish, while others struggle to keep pace or ultimately fail (Figure 1.2).

The impact of influence reaches far beyond business networks and robotics. It works at a low-level dynamic layer, where countless framing gently guides us to specific decisions. It's a place of developing minds, not yet made-up opinions or choices—and therefore, the best subject

Figure 1.2 The path ahead

to rounds of influence. Consider it the same as the interaction between magnets with many positive and negative forces—powerful forces of our life's context that shape and drive our myriad decisions. Let's say you want to lose weight but have a weak spot for fried foods and beer. Rest assured: you are not alone—it's a perpetual battle between the desire for a healthy life and urges for indulgent goodies. A fight we can win with the help of AI's untapped potential.

AI can provide a human-level intermediary layer, guiding polarized wishes of the "in-between" state and supporting motivations to keep life and balance indulgences. AI's support is but a nudge, something to "predictably alter behavior without forbidding option"[2] in the direction of choices toward a healthier path. Consider the equalized state of perfect balance, where every scenario can be easily navigated. Always at equilibrium, we'd crush complications and walk confidently, standing as a resilient badass while navigating weight loss. Even if our course is pure to start, it continues to grow in complexity, and the world tugs at reality again.

AI sits at the crossroads of intention and reality, cleverly expanding technology's reach and enriching our human experience. AI can embody our choices, values, and evolutionary potential. Efficiency, yes, but more so the way it ultimately molds behavior. It holds the promise of forward momentum and provides solutions that harness technological power to navigate a far more complex world with diverse human interests forever in play. Beyond a business tool, it's an ally in our busy lives. It's not all perfect; AI's power is a double-edged sword. The same AI that empowers can subtly shape.

Influence Design in the AI Era: Business strategy will explore various mindsets, techniques, and strategies from interactive discussions around advanced technical adoption. Foundational to this work is influence architecture, as the pieces that support influence with AI are orig-inal, underground, varied, and ethically supportive—a unique art that prioritizes safety and well-being, even when influence conflicts with desires. Influence with AI requires a profound understanding of alignment and provides extensive, adaptable, and relevant supporting context. Influence architecture comprises the organization's distinctive strategy and practices for cultivating desired behavior in and beyond the AI era. It involves leveraging data, AI, situational awareness, deployed machines, and human ingenuity to shape decision-making processes and includes frameworks for supporting interactions with internal and external audiences.

Picture this: you walk past your favorite coffee shop on the way to work, and a message of support for your exhausting day pops up on your smartwatch with a coupon for your favorite caffeinated drink. More than witnessing the interaction, you are participating in an example of influence supported by an organization's influence archi-tecture: AI (code, data, model), situational awareness (path forward), contextual support (what's happening), accessibility (via mobile phone), and motionless interactions (recommendation that supports you) drive much-needed support for the day ahead. A win-win scenario, it merely underscores the magic of AI as a compass for easy and enjoyable living.

Here's where the artistry of influence comes in: Real-time interac-tions shape behavior and promote mutually agreed-upon benefits over time. As a new pattern becomes established, discounts will gradually decrease, making ordering ahead standard practice. Your new favourite coffee shop can adjust staff to make more coffee and take fewer orders at the counter.

Do you align with this proactive mindset?

Is your organization actively adopting this forward-thinking approach?

Excitement for AI can lead organizations to rush headlong into implementation without careful consideration. Some might add AI elements to existing strategies rather than thoughtfully crafting an AI strategy aligned with needs. Before chasing the promise of influence, it's crucial to understand your organization's analytical maturity level, not in the traditional form of how the organization thinks of or describes maturity but in observation of actual organizational behavior. Continuous self-evaluation is essential for successfully navigating the modern landscape of influence design. By strategically and creatively using digital platforms and adequately understanding data capabilities, the organization can shape perceptions, drive engagement, and inspire action that nourishes behavior.

Considering AI often involves identifying specific use cases and interactions to improve, like adding AI elements to existing strategies. At a granular focus, It might cultivate a sense of growing control over external factors. However, actual influence stems from continuous, long-term guidance, maintaining constant alignment with a strategic vision. While managing individual interactions might seem simple, scaling these efforts across an organization's complex structures and touchpoints can be challenging. Quite honestly, giving decisional support to the organization's edge is a nightmare scenario for executive leadership and is the most significant and ignored hurdle to overcome.

While AI offers immense potential, it also poses significant challenges. Successfully integrating AI requires more than simply assigning AI tasks to existing roles. Organizations need proactive leadership in concert with a deep understanding of AI throughout the workforce, not just a superficial awareness. A new role emerges to address the need for an influential leader and organizational champion: the influence architect. A nontraditional leader, a unique kind of artist, owns the organization's influence architecture and spearheads AI integration, ensuring alignment with the organization's goals and enhancing existing strengths.

Like chess grandmasters, they analyze the landscape before making strategically aligned, long-term recommendations, decipher the organization's hidden connections, and guide bold moves to achieve alignment. From continuous investigation, deep knowledge enables the smooth integration of AI, boosting existing organizational strengths.

Bridging business and technology, the influence architect is a strategist and translator. They decipher complex AI workflows into actionable plans, equipping teams to understand and leverage AI alongside expertise. They foster a culture of collaborative intelligence where all forms of data-driven insights are accessible, understood, supported with context, and utilized.

AI adoption holds the potential for understandable and remarkable success or unforeseen failure in the competitive landscape. The organization's influence architect navigates a delicate balance, prioritizing responsible and ethical AI implementation. As a visionary leader charting invisible forces, they empower the entire organization to thrive in the complex world of AI. With an unwavering focus on alignment, influence architects ensure every action propels the organization toward long-term success.

Organizational Influence

Entities of all forms, whether profit-driven corporations or cause-driven organizations, hold considerable capacities to impact society in numerous pervasive ways. Multifaceted determinations, coordinated initiatives, and even public stances on societal issues often emanate far-reaching consequences. "Choosing to support a social cause is frequently a tightrope walk for businesses, filled with potential rewards and risks. The public backlash, polarizing views, and potential damage to a company's reputation can be daunting."[3]

A social media platform's algorithm, designed to captivate, can insidiously mold cultural precedents, while a trade group's strategic lobbying exploits may subtly warp legislation to their advantage.

Influential corporations frequently leverage lobbying or backing for preferred candidates to shape economies, directives, and political terrains. Moreover, cultural and advocacy associations actively endeavor to steer public opinion. Technology titans, as current events exhibit, can cunningly affect how we interact and behave through their innovative designs. Lastly, industrial operations unavoidably impose enormous environmental effects, touching nearby communities and the worldwide environment in material ways. Comprehending how diverse entities operate and wield influence remains crucial for navigating a complicated world with discernment.

In simpler words, organizations' power over people is no new phenomenon. It has always been about ethical dilemmas concerning how far research can go and who should own the objective of keeping societal welfare on an equal footing.[4] Traditionally, at an organizational level, influence has been guided by the organization's philosophy and leadership desires. Looking ahead, AI-powered leadership can plan for and exert influence driven by machines. Early opportunities for machine-driven influence should focus on simple and modular problems in closed systems. Longer-term opportunities will come after experience, including complex scenarios influencing decision-making processes in open environments.

Organizations will shift from broad, centralized AI models to smaller, specialized models tailored to specific tasks as AI usage extends outward, integrating into the organizational fabric. This change leads to precise AI applications where context, awareness, timing, and influence align perfectly, elevating AI from a whimsical oddity to the scarier "aware and learning machine" part. Setting aside "scary" brings a focus on achieving harmony between tech innovation and ethical concerns, making AI fully comply with human values and benefit society. In an increasingly AI-driven world, leaders are part of the broader societal conversation about how technology impacts our communities and people, not just what impact it might have on a specific product or service. By addressing problems head-on, we can tap the potential of AI for good and work toward a humanity-centric IT future.

Reflecting and strategizing about influence empowers an organization to survive over the longer term. Itemizing influence effort begins with implementing a generic portfolio-level classification of AI. One that is easily recognized, memorized, and reused. It should be organizationally relevant but can be as simple as categorizing AI as before the interaction (pre), after the interaction (post), or during. In addition, the development of AI in numerous areas leads us to revitalize our commitment: should we always consider whether, for a given effort, AI is indeed nothing but an ever-present tool that more effortlessly manipulates decisions and responses?

Initial models may change over time (also considering the business expansion, other processes, and additional AI initiatives) from an influential phase of "enhancing interaction for improvement" to a mere automated one that will define how things are done now, or better said, in alignment with changing times, where it takes place—"how things ought to be done."

The future of powerful AI brings new challenges, and as such, organizations must carefully evaluate AI and its potential risks, creating "influence policies" to manage evolving situations. Executive-driven conversations on policy are essential for cultivating responsible AI development across the organization. They can also significantly advance responsible functioning, enabling the organization to use AI across its

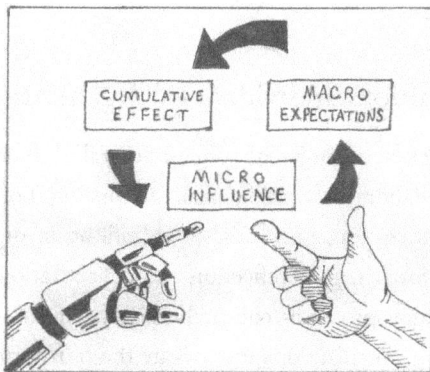

Figure 1.3 The influential hand of AI and the invisible hand of economics

total agility, hence providing trust for reliable deployment of AI (Figure 1.3).

Classical economic theory, like Adam Smith's "invisible hand," suggests that self-interest drives individuals in a free market, ultimately benefiting society.[5] However, the rise of AI, with its potentially vast influence, poses a new challenge. If concentrated in the hands of a few influential individuals or organizations, AI could shift the balance away from individual freedoms and overall societal well-being. It further highlights the extended need for proactive classification and regulation to ensure long-term sustainability. Remember, there is no "opt-out" to influence.

For the successful few that hold epic proportions, the increasing dominance of AI in both commerce and society will inevitably require reexamining long-held assumptions about antitrust policy and fair competition. Traditional remedies intended to dethrone monopolies, like compelling the severing of divisions, may prove toothless against corporations whose primacy stems essentially from intellectual resources. Consider Amazon, whose supremacy in the retail realm stems from a synthesis of automation and machine learning that undergirds the entire operation. Unbundling algorithms and data structures force dissociation. Would Amazon retain the edge, permitting such transcendence over rivals in the first place? There's a wide array of issues surrounding the oversight of entities fueled principally by advances in AI, necessitating innovative solutions to safeguard dynamism and parity in an economy increasingly ruled by code.[6]

Cognition: Individual to Organizational

The advent of AI necessitates an organizational shift from individual cognition to collaborative intelligence, embracing both human and machine capabilities. Organizations should adopt an organization-centric perspective, fostering self-reflection and collaboration to understand the decision-making processes comprehensively. Continuous self-reflection will empower organizations to navigate the transformative effects of AI with greater control and confidence.

Adam Smith's "invisible hand" takes on new dimensions in the AI era. Historically, individual choices inadvertently contributed to social and organizational benefits.[5] With the advent of AI, intentional influence by machines in support of individuals or organizations has become a reality, marking a significant moment where personal goals intersect with purposefully crafted digital influence, shaping the decision-making landscape. In the context of AI, the "influential hand" refers to the unseen impact of AI on individual and organizational decisions, expanding the traditional understanding of the concept.

AI's influential force compels us to master our autonomy, so the journey reshapes human–AI relationships into a collaboration based on mutualism. From a mutualistic stance, collaboration symbolizes our unity as human beings and a testament to our resilience in the face of an emerging machine force. Within the organization, an individual's alignment is distinct as an employee, in a role, on a team, or elsewhere in the organizational structure. Individuals fulfill specific roles and adhere to the organization's management procedures. Going beyond individual self-cognition to nourish managerial cognition, it's imperative to distinguish between understanding the broader organizational context and simply knowing how to perform our jobs.

To expand management mindsets, leaders in support of shifting workflows worry less about the granular group-level specifics to put more stress on the big-picture cross-organizational interactions of the organization. A complete systematic view enables employees to understand the big picture and think beyond role activities, recognizing their place in line supporting the organization. Leadership can nourish alignment by directly exposing metrics through a business intelligence stack, enabling individual team members to measure against contributions. "When people have conflicting priorities or unclear, meaningless, or arbitrarily shifting goals, they become frustrated, cynical, and demotivated."[7] Leaders can continue playing a pivotal role in fostering a proactive culture by rolling out methodologies like Objective and Key Results (OKRs) for goal setting. Customizing OKRs to each role and aligning with organization initiatives contribute to a more proactive culture that aligns personal aspirations with collective goals. Such internal influence on the organization's direction furthers the leader's alignment as an integral part of the organization's success.

Beyond direct team alignment, leaders who cross functional boundaries can expose numerous opportunities and gather insights on processes, guidelines, and best practices. Cultivating individual awareness, fostering collaborative efforts, and harnessing advanced technological tools provide a robust framework for effective decision making and performance evaluation. To prepare and advance the organization, equip business, and technical professionals with a deep understanding of AI principles, including basic statistical literacy and business decision science.

Diverse Paths and Multiple Truths

I take pride in having successfully spearheaded AI initiatives during the tumultuous period of the global pandemic. My leadership extended to various organizations, including a prominent top three global bank, one of the largest for-profit health care systems in the United States, and even contracts with the U.S. federal government. Emerging in late 2019, the pandemic hit swiftly and intensely. From the outset, it was clear that leadership needed to go beyond merely "flattening the curve" and proactively prepare for potential future waves of infection. Rather than remaining idle and waiting, it was time to actively prepare for the inevitable challenges ahead. It was a massive revelation for everyone how rapidly the spread of a virus could be compounded, particularly by those who aren't naturally inclined to think exponentially. More importantly, it was time to actively acknowledge resolving more than one "curve." The implications were huge, and they multiplied quickly. Simple tactics like social distancing reduced the spread but increased pressure on individuals to make behavioral changes contrary to lifelong learning.

Many articles argued that predictive insights were worthless because all models could be described as broken and unusable because they did not have enough data.[8] On the other hand, COVID-focused predictive efforts opened and gained importance as they were necessary to understand what was happening.[9]

The push to discredit predictive modeling arose from a combination of factors: a lack of understanding about the potential benefits of creating meaningful scenarios, a failure to recognize the power of impactful storytelling, and a tendency to selectively promote only certain narratives related to AI. Even the opening of one article leans directly toward avoidance: "The COVID-19 pandemic has lessened the efficacy of predictive models, regardless of the algorithmic approach that built them, to the point that they may now be counterproductive."[10]

Despite random exogenous events that change behavior "overnight," long-term trends seen in the past can still suggest patterns of ingrained habits and potential future actions. Ingrained habits exposed in predictive scenarios can help inform what may or may not happen, even if the exact events are unclear. Having situational knowledge brings robust understanding, supports faster decisions, and allows the organization to adapt faster to change.

For those new to machine learning and predictive modeling, it's an important reminder that the field is constantly evolving. These days, data scientists engage heavily in curating the raw materials and perform many statistical modeling experiments to discover patterns and relationships—extensive efforts to find the "best fit" model representing patterns in the data. Because machine learning algorithms are adaptable, they can participate in a broad spectrum of tasks. They can tackle binary classification, answering questions with a simple yes/no or multiclass classification, where the data are split into low, medium, and high groups. They can also do regression analysis by fitting a line or curve to data points and use time series methods to analyze temporal changes in data.

Modern machine learning is exciting because automation rapidly tries multiple approaches simultaneously and sees which fits best. With excellent tools and techniques for data scientists to automatically build models (check out DataRobot.com), the burden of relying on prebuilt and often misaligned capabilities is reduced. Decreased development time allows data scientists to focus on fine-tuning models for individual data sets, giving precise and vital predictions. Although out-of-the-box models provide us with a kickstart, the beauty behind automated machine learning is that it allows for a more responsive way of approaching problems by keeping your data focused. Actual muscle comes from an "everything-on-repeat" automated process that puts the burden of testing and refining models until they're as good as they will ever be, squeezing every drop of value out of your data.

It's worth clarifying that the "models" are not static objects. They are developed through an iterative process of exploring the best-fit statistical methods and algorithms for the uniqueness of data. Models depend on specific, recurring patterns or characteristics within your data set to perform well. To put it differently, while prebuilt models can be beneficial in starting your exploration, the real impact would arise from creating and testing (and then improving) more complex experiments, highly tuned to extract as much value from the data as possible and achieve better results. Instead of relying solely on prebuilt models that may not be nuanced enough to capture the uniqueness of your data and problem, a dynamic approach lets you:

Adapt to data: An active approach keeps your models in line with the freshest dynamics, ensuring their relevance and accuracy.

Discover hidden relationships: Using different algorithms and techniques, we can discover those subtle relationships or patterns that an out-of-the-box model might overlook.

Optimize for specific goals: Your business model is unique; your models should be adjusted accordingly to optimize against those objectives (good customer retention and sales predictions combined with efficient supply chain order management).

Make models interpretable: Understanding the factors driving predictions leads to better decision making and explains the outcomes you produce to stakeholders.

Relentless pursuit of the "right" answer and the singular "path forward" often clouds the vision of the richness of unexplored paths and alternative truths. Recall that a model is not a piece of code; it's an organism that grows with the passage of data through its veins. Adopt the iterative approach to building models; you will unveil insights hiding in plain sight. Overlooking the nuances between paths and truths hinders our capacity to navigate complexities effectively. It's time to close the gap and adopt a more tactical approach to information analysis, recognizing the wealth of insights concealed within diverse perspectives. A nuanced understanding is not just valuable; it's inspiring and will continue to be invaluable as we navigate future challenges and evolving behaviors in organizational aspirations! To simplify, explore diverse paths and frame multiple truths.

The Artistry of AI Teams

The term "influencer" has recently mutated beyond its original meaning; it is primarily defined by a figure who utilizes social media platforms to create fashions, movements, and trends. Modern influencers are almost entirely characterized by their online presence in the digital era. They own content creation and deliver top-notch quality that is well received by their audience, which engages them. Many influencers are situated in particular niches, aspiring to be professionals in their craft. The most successful are early adopters of the latest tools, treating their online presence with a business-like mindset and trying for commercial acumen—even when it comes to deals—as well as negotiating partnerships on an ad hoc basis and using data analytics in decisions. Although it has no bearing on industry or society standards for the philosophy of their brand, credibility, and trust are fundamental in creating a durable connection between influencers and the public.

From the individual to the organization, the focus shifts to organizational influence and the transformative role of "influence architects." Currently operating without this title in multiple roles, AI-savvy professionals are reshaping how organizations operate. Unlike social media influencers who seek external attention, influence architects work strategically within an organization as guardians of influential solutions. They focus on orchestrating synchronized influence and interactions across departments, navigating complex technologies, and ensuring AI alignment with organizational goals, ethics, and responsible use.

Influence architects hold executive oversight (indeed authority) when formally placed into an organization, yet they execute with an interactive edge mentality. As progressive leaders, they focus on internal stakeholders and optimizing processes between departments to support macro-organizational behavior and micro-organizational influences.

In comparison, traditional influencers rely heavily on charm and social media to convince their external audiences. On the other hand, influence architects focus on behaviors that drive positive return on investment (ROI) and tend to gear toward an impact, fostering internal and external relationships, operational excellence, and ethical considerations for AI usage within the organization.

AI team members become the brushstrokes on this canvas of organizational hopes in our ever-changing environment. They create more than algorithms and models: they design the artifacts that weave into human behaviors. As artists paint with emotion, the AI stemming from an organization is a design intervention whose content forges and fits into organizational cultural rhythms—no longer limited to the technical domain. That goes into psychology and even sociology, paying attention to how humans do things and designing AI-based solutions that work harmoniously with what already exists.

Of course, it takes a high degree of collaboration on an individual team—but at some point, it's evolution and nothing more, for there may never be anything better; we are addressing human dynamics and behavior within organizations. It contrasts the strict frameworks of regulation or prescription that, as servants to human needs, are more gently custodians trying to guide people and teams on the same page with long-term goals. It's a gentle waltz of understanding, predicting, and moderating that is fine-tuned at the moment of execution by the efforts of AI teams based on real-time feedback. In this model, AI is no longer a software or a capability; it is an active agent.

If properly orchestrated, your AI team is the most critical enabler to drive organizational change. Oversight spans product managers, line of business (LOB) leaders, and senior executives bridging the technical and commercial worlds. The mix of positions in executive leadership and corresponding duties prevents a holistic organizational understanding (micro to macro, vice versa, and everything in between), raising the question of how the organization's consciousness is regulated in society.

Realizing that your organization has a distinctive way of seeing the world and engaging with reality is essential and needs to be embedded in every element of AI produced. The organization's attitude is embodied in company mission statements, visions, and leadership approaches. Ultimately, organizational culture influences how leadership and the workforce approach problems and seek solutions to help accomplish goals (Figure 1.4).

Advocating for a collaborative approach to AI integration means fostering small micro-influences that drive significant macro-behavioral changes, and a conspicuous absence of oversight exists regarding such consequential shifts. Even more so, there's a shortage of executives monitoring how evolving behavioral changes at the micro-level align with and cultivate the macro-organizational "consciousness." Strategies are often dictated from the top, but it's the actions on the ground that truly drive results.

Envision an AI artist, a visionary who shapes and nurtures the creative spirit of your AI team. Their discerning eye ensures that the AI's output resonates with users, fostering positive and meaningful interactions within and beyond the organization's walls. As your formally declared influence architect, they navigate the complex landscape of AI initiatives, overseeing how they affect the organization's overall approach to AI (its consciousness). The ideal candidate excels at understanding both business needs and technical implementations. They can research, document, and translate between these worlds, bridging the

Figure 1.4 Find the proper influence

gap between business workflows and technical strategies within your AI team.

Zooming in and out, they understand broad strategies (macro) and critical detail (micro)—and how they interconnect to influence the organization's entire approach to AI. Unlike AI business strategists, who should maintain expertise and focus on specific business segments, the influence architect takes a holistic view. They guide the entire AI team in interacting with the organization, overseeing tactical strategies, and promoting positive organizational behavioral changes. Essentially, the influence architect orchestrates a nuanced approach to influence behaviors, shaping the organization's future with AI.

Embedding AI and Influence Architects

Building the ranks of influential architects, either named or tasked, is an emerging opportunity. As AI logic permeates various workflows and innovation flourishes, influence architects serve as the vital link, aligning critical components with overarching business strategy and ensuring that AI seamlessly integrates into relevant processes, executing influence at the right moments. As skilled conductors, they harmonize business acumen, technical expertise, and interpersonal skills within the organizational structure.

Just as you would create a symphony, each part of AI reasoning fits into the whole. Complex and distributed integration embeds AI in the lifeblood of organizational processes. Using knowledge, they ensure implementation is tied to the fabric of organizational life and directly influences outcomes according to strategies on a business-wide scale.

To a broader extent, using an orchestrated tool from the AI team reduces external unpredictability and increases desirability. More importantly, through the thoughtful incorporation of AI in operations, architects can help shape events rather than react to them, serving as a more constructive and effective form of interaction. For example, in a customer service scenario, AI can also listen to live inbound call activities (such as caller voice and emotions). Armed with this information, AI helpfully tweaks the call script on the fly to equip agents with answers that calm tensions, personalize interactions, and drive more positive customer experiences.

The influence architect's vision is a nuanced but anticipatory view. Like foresight to a chess grandmaster: a dance of interplay between data and algorithms that becomes art for any architect fluent in the nuances of timing and precision. Achieving sophistication, businesses can effortlessly sail a future in which AI becomes an ethereal presence, guiding itself calmly into the predetermined directions instead of what could be volatile, disruptive atmospherics within the industry.

Strategically Embedded Artificial Logic

The architects' influence transforms an AI technology strategy into a symphony. Precision and timing touch on readiness for an outcome determined well in advance. Below are a series of framing concepts for strategically embedding artificial logic in support of influence:

Form and function: Content is like the canvas of digital influence, while sound curation becomes a brushstroke behind it. In the same way influencers, brands, and content creators meticulously curate their media to deliver high-quality visuals, organizations can utilize generative AI to create attractive graphics, presentations, books, documents like PDFs with noticeable visualizations to interactive ones, and even videos. The key is in a seamless and unhindered cocktail of entertainment aligned with bursts of information, which creates the right mix that triggers an emotional resonance with your target audience.

Delivery mediums: Coexistence with the digital world, everything connected and awake. Through technology, digital platforms are potential canvases for influencing through curated content or an entirely larger-than-life experience. Where Instagram visually drives content, Twitter, or X as it's named now, takes one messaging sentence similarly. Every platform is a different canvas, allowing organizations to paint their art according to the palette of each specific audience.

Uniqueness and reach: Uniqueness and reach refer to the themes, values, or aesthetics an organization aligns with by building a brand and giving life to its identity—uniqueness is appealing. With a little more personalization, authenticity, and relatability, organizations can broaden their audience. This has been done explicitly through organizational taglines/slogans and can go on to add more to the organization's essence and identity. AI is expanding the organization's reach by allowing for customization and personalization at the individual level, leading to more unique and impactful interactions.

Interactions: While interactions can alter the path triggered by fate, influencing well is a delicate balance. The art makes the influence seem steady but allows interactions to change. The right balance is essential; too much intervention or too little influence to change the course of events will lead to less-than-optimal results and can be detrimental. Organizations can become capable of improvisation in interpersonal dynamics and engaging with influence, seamlessly turning observers into participants.

Insight: More data-driven influence in an era ruled by information allows persuasion and alignment to become more precise. It's worth accepting "data" as synonymous with "information," understanding that data with no context is not informative. Analyzing information enables an organization to penetrate deep into the context to generate growth and knowledge, elements needed for situational awareness. Further, this process can also be extended to making a prediction or correlating the root cause, giving invaluable insights into issue resolution/process-flow refactoring.

Amplification and scale: By collaborating, kindred organizations join forces as essential brushstrokes in creating a connected tapestry. On this expanded whole, commonality offers each piece new avenues for standing out further. Digital, social, and informational networks are the middle fabric of influence, driving beyond individual or organizational efforts. Ideally, amplification can work by providing an optional service that extends and increases a message—or your product or marketing campaign to make it even more effective. In contrast, scale is related to an operation's actual size and efficiency—including production volumes, market footprint, or general organizational girth. Scalability in this context would refer to the whole process of streamlining and improving processes, making them faster than ever with more bang for the buck.

Alignment: In support of the long-term focus, if you are looking for a catchphrase of sufficient gravity to describe what matters most in how we behave as an organization and how tomorrow takes shape, it's alignment. Influence thrives on innovation and adaptability. Adopting advanced approaches, patterns, interactive flow, and technologies ensures that the lobes provide dynamically fresh influence opportunities. When organizations embrace creativity during times of change, they open up opportunities to influence the direction of that change. Leveraging predictive analytics can act as a guiding light, providing data-driven out-in-front insights that help align the entire organization toward common goals. Think of AI's role in influence as a form of bumpers on either side to defend against going off course. Either way, with or without risk, bumpers keep your company on target and nudge back toward success.

Cautious restraint: Ultimately, every business success strategy comes down to a version of self-discipline. Operating AI within a managed framework is essential, showing great restraint. Balancing strategic activities and authentic levels of engagement builds trust with stakeholders. Efforts need to be regular, and "impactful initiatives" should also be opportunities for structured engagement in human terms. Although the desired results are defined, they must uplift and inspire. As an organization, endless endurance comes from the idea of perpetual restraint. Its value is to appreciate and reinforce current conditions and support the creation of flexible designs for future changes where development can evolve into the plan. Although cautious restraint is easy to grasp, it's often the hardest for us to practice.

Influencing Tomorrow

Influential digital art emerges amidst social media wars, heated political chatter, and share-worthy online videos. Creative work that blends strategic thinking, insights into human behavior, and cutting-edge code to reach across physical and social barriers, ensuring interactions genuinely make an impact. Skilled AI teams can craft compelling narratives, enrich user behaviors, and sculpt influence within organizations with precision and nuance. They leave their mark on the digital landscape through accuracy, contributing significantly to the intricate web of artificial sway. Unlike the hidden forces of traditional markets, the "artificial hand" of AI processes data openly, adjusting to shifting factors. Over time, people may fail to realize how their environment and interactions are subtly nudging based on the Organization's unique influence architecture.

CHAPTER 2

Analytical Maturity

Mind the Gap

Is the fast-paced evolution of AI creating a widening analytical maturity gap, outpacing us and leaving a growing need to catch up?

In the ever-evolving world of technology, staying informed about the latest advancements is a constant challenge and comes with an ongoing assessment of our analytical capabilities. Even when we think we're keeping up, the rapid pace of progress can leave us unexpectedly behind. With the constant evolution of data analysis tools, it's critical to assess our analytical skills regularly. Pressure to stay ahead can generate a sense of urgency, leading to questions such as:

Regarding data comprehension—Can we effectively interpret the nuances of advanced data analysis and extract meaningful insights?

Ensuring data reliability—Can we trust the integrity and accuracy of our data sources?

Focusing on relevance—Are the data-driven predictions and insights applicable to our circumstances and challenges?

Considering AI's autonomy—Will we be able to use generative AI tools independently, or will we always require step-by-step guidance?

Reflection provides an opportunity to evaluate organizational maturity to stay ahead of the curve. Well before the organization, it starts with individuals. Take a moment and dive into analyzing everyday thinking. Upon careful reflection, you'll discover natural intuition is impressive and accurate. Individuals effortlessly describe events, predict

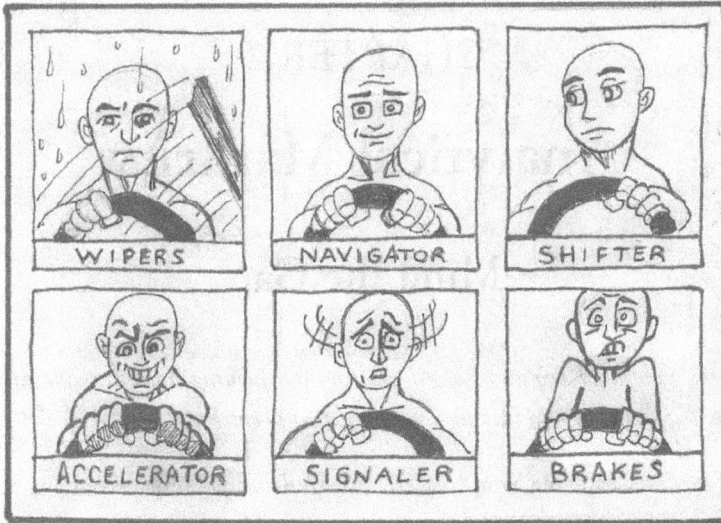

Figure 2.1 On the organizational journey, everyone's in the driver's seat

outcomes, and find solutions—for themselves and others. While these skills serve well in daily life, unlocking the power of extensive complex data requires a new level of analytical thinking, primarily when data are spread across multiple systems, services, and teams. Going beyond intuitive thinking, grasping a complete understanding, and analyzing and leveraging extensive information (data) can also be a powerful motivator to align individuals to the organization.

The good news is that humans excel in seamless and mature analytical thinking as functional organisms within the expansive universe. That said, anticipating a diverse range of responses influenced by personal experience, organizational maturity, and situational focus, the question arises: Can an organization match this level of individual proficiency (Figure 2.1)?

From an organizational perspective, achieving maturity with AI is like having multiple drivers navigate a maze together. While possible, getting everyone on the same page is challenging. Even when fully aligned, how do we move forward without getting caught up in all the hype?

It's worth restarting on common ground, focusing on organizational growth, and comparing it to a straightforward representative model. The Analytical Maturity Model, introduced by Gartner in 2016, is a valuable guide for understanding how companies can evolve with data-driven insights.[11] The model outlines a phased approach toward complete optimization, advancing from one type of analysis to the next. As illustrated, analytical maturity is an organization's progression to enhance its ability to extract supportive insights from data. Briefly exploring these steps is valuable, as they are commonly called the analytical maturity journey.

The first step, descriptive analytics, is the starting phase, where organizations rely on historical data to identify and describe what has happened. Examples of descriptive analytics can be seen in plain old reports, dashboards, and data visualization, such as creating sales performance reports, customer demographics, website traffic analysis, and so on.

The second step, diagnostic analytics, further explains why such things happen. Organizations get more than details on events; they analyze and diagnose the causes of those events. Examining the factors driving an increase or decrease in sales and the primary drivers contributing to customer attrition is helpful in diagnostic instances.

Moving further, organizations attempt to predict **what could happen**, that is, predictive analytics (third stage). In the AI era, this is where the true magic of statistical analysis can be seen—forward-looking information. Models of statistics as machine learning algorithms can predict future trends or results based on signals from historical data. Organizations can more accurately forecast future sales, demand, and potential high-value customers—allowing for greater insight and planning in decision making.

If you can anticipate the future, you can suggest actions to steer it toward what is most desired. Our next and last level is called Prescriptive Analytics. Enterprises envision what will happen and **make actionable recommendations** to leverage the results. The most mature organizations can use prescriptive analytics to recommend tailored marketing strategies for segmented customers and optimize supply chain logistics and efficiency.

Moving through these stages signals an enterprise's evolution in analytic maturity, from understanding historical trends to achieving predictions that shape future outcomes. All stages reinforce the next, and higher-maturity organizations create more value than those with lower maturity.

On the one hand, human judgment seems less complex and much more seamless than the Analytical Maturity Model. No one says aloud to themselves, "I will now decide something"; instead, we make decisions effortlessly. On the other hand, the Analytical Maturity Model segregates seamless pieces of human thinking. Daily decisions are based on intuition and personal experiences, fundamentally different from an Analytical Maturity Model's structured, linear progression. This juxtaposition highlights how far advanced human thinking is from the complicated decision-making processes within an organization. Personal encounters, feelings, and distinct biases often lead to individual preferences. As complex systems, organizations must traverse multiple layers of opinions, leadership styles, cultures, and objectives. It represents a very different way of *thinking* at a broad scale and demands more rigorous effort.

A critical maturity gap stems from the crucial distinction of individual versus organizational decision making, and leaders must reflect on the fundamental differences to bridge the gap. By recognizing the organization's unique entities and meeting at the current level of maturity, leaders can develop thought processes that effectively connect the personal and organizational, paving the way for more impactful solutions.

Analytical Proficiency: From Observation to Action

Advancing through the different levels of Gartner's model marks growth in analytical maturity: understanding what happened and why, making predictions, and proactivity in influencing future outcomes. Every stage depends on curated information from the previous one. Organizations at a higher level of maturity leverage data to achieve additional agility in decision making and create competitive separation from industry brethren.

Seldom does a vision fit into one word. Occasionally, the most ordinary words become icons of a new quantum leap—take *Apple*, for example. In a sense, *alignment* is a one-word vision for the theme of influence design in the AI era. More than a term, it applies to every facet of an organization—a guiding principle toward shared goals. Alignment is a compelling concept for being analytically proficient—the difference between making observations and turning those into actionable insights that align well with up-and-coming events.

Alignment clarifies historical events leading to ideal futures, a course for reaching and defining success. Furthermore, strategic alignment represents the degree to which an organization is mature in making data and insights actionable, more easily accessible, and seamlessly support-ing decision making and growth. As a simple word with significant consequences, it resonates like a well-played symphony, each section perfectly aligned as an interactive masterpiece. The better aligned, the more substantial and lasting the outcomes. Unfortunately, we navi-gate without a precise map, and success rarely follows a linear path. Hindsight can also deceive us; perceived setbacks might be necessary course corrections, as even the "wrong" turns could be inaccurate attempts to align with goals.

Momentum and success in collaborative intelligence are much more than cooperation and require a view of varied perspectives: human and machine. What seems evident to one human may not be apparent if shared with another. Likewise, machines have minimal instructions to focus models, understand information, and account for actual context, both their own and that of the environment.

Consider a model trained to interpret customer feedback. If the model is trained over data that reflect one demographic/region, it may be hard to learn the input nuances from another culture. Similarly, a human analyst may need more domain expertise to understand data fully. The analyst's fallibility poses a grave risk to the accuracy and fairness of the model. Missed details or misinterpretations can perpet-uate discriminatory practices or lead to erroneous business decisions.

Hence, there is a need for rigorous oversight and validation to mitigate the potential negative consequences of human error on AI's performance. So, to reach the proper contextual level, organizations need to expand efforts to include a common, or rather—standard, contextual understanding of all models, including but not limited to:

Data diversity: Ensuring the AI's training data encompasses various perspectives, demographics, and scenarios to avoid discriminatory outcomes.

Clear communication: Establishing effective communication channels supports the model to enable humans and machines to express doubts, ask questions, and exchange information, promoting transparency and understanding.

Contextual awareness: Designing AI models that grasp the broader context of a situation, moving beyond isolated contexts to dynamic situational awareness.

Human-in-the-loop: Integrating human intervention into AI systems to identify and correct potential errors, biases, and unintended consequences.

Continuous learning: Encouraging ongoing learning and adaptation in humans and machines to refine their knowledge, skills, and understanding of the evolving context.

By cultivating shared languages and perspectives, the bounty of collective intelligence remains within our grasp, enabling humans to align with intelligent machines toward common objectives. A significant challenge lies in the difference between individual and organizational analytical maturity. Even with a top-notch AI team, expertise must align with critical initiatives, bridging the gap with a comprehensive approach that seamlessly integrates business and technology functions.

Chances are, you've witnessed a car accident at some point, and thankfully, your experience helps provide context to the seamless extent of human thinking. As a focus, we're concerned with the motion of events, not necessarily the accident itself. It's certainly not a cue to hit the brakes and rubberneck at the next accident you see. It is, however, a chance to focus on the seamless thinking of individuals (Figure 2.2).

Figure 2.2 Insights ahead

Picture yourself as the motorist en route to a coffee shop for that overdue injection. On our regular path, looking forward to that added jolt of an enjoyable libation, you suddenly see a few cars up with their hazards on, meaning your standard journey is anything but. So, what goes on in that mind at this point:

Brake lights are on two cars ahead, and one car puts on its hazard.

Without giving thought to execution, you quickly move on to descriptive analytics. As you creep toward the accident, watching other cars swerve around, insights get more specific:

One car's back bumper is dangling; it looks like it was hit from behind. The traffic light up ahead is still flashing; therefore, the light's out, and someone was not paying attention.

By correctly diagnosing the problem, thinking has set into diagnostic analytics mode. Within milliseconds, you understand that the second car wasn't paying attention—a minor insight win. Before you celebrate, your thoughts kick in again with a reminder that you're still driving a car. Processing incident-based data, a new issue emerges:

It looks like this was due to the lack of power at the traffic light. The driver must have been following too closely ... and wasn't paying attention. I'm following a car. How close am I to that car? Are they slowing down?

Based on a rapid assessment of the situation and more details coming to light, thinking moves into another dimension:

I could be next. The light is still out. I must keep space between my vehicle and the vehicle ahead.

By now, mental processing has jumped into predictive analytics, resulting from all the descriptive and diagnostic facts. All before that perfect cup of Java and your elevating caffeine! Coming closer to the accident, a last act of oration occurs:

I'm slowing down. I need my coffee. I am focused and will pay attention to the road and all the other cars moving around me.

Fully informed with rich context, position, and available actions, you slow down and allow a safe distance. By taking additional steps, like turning down the radio, staying on high alert, and remaining focused, you've come full circle into analytic maturity, avoiding potential problems. It's simple, yet mimicking the same behavior across an entire organization is tricky. Why the disconnect?

Dealing with an organization includes other team members, large amounts of information, many ideas, and different goals. Scaling up seamless individual intuitive thinking in organizations seems impossible. What makes individual decisions so powerful—fast, flexible, and contextual understanding—all require much more support applied at scale. Due to diverse histories and personal experiences, people can swiftly learn new analytic methods, but transforming these solitary triumphs into an organization-wide approach takes time. The key resides in recognizing and relating individual analytic abilities with a shared organizational mentality. Preserving a balance between personal innovation and collective strength is essential for a healthy, high-performing ecosystem.

The "Thin Wide Line"

We Work Together and Sit Next to Each Other, but We're So Far Apart (Figure 2.3).

Upon arriving at the office one morning, one of my workmates, an experienced and very high-performing person responsible for taking customer calls, stopped by my desk. He said hello and asked if I would help him with his computer, as it showed three colored bars (red–blue–green) along with the message "No Sync Input." It made me pause, and after thinking about it, I realized that the computer's signal was not reaching the monitor. It felt strange to be hesitant; however, with

Figure 2.3 The thin wide line: Two perspectives, two realities

the straightforward nature of my job, it gave me pause that I would have to get down on all fours and inspect wiring under a desk. Sitting at his workstation, I noticed the computer's power light was off. I was delighted to know it could be resolved without crawling under the desk. Pressing power, fingers crossed, the machine started, and I confidently announced, "Here you go, all good." My somewhat ashamed colleague shrugged and said, "Ah, thank you."

Have you ever forgotten to turn something on or off? Ahh, remember the days when "reboot" was an actual solution!?!

Returning to my workstation, I realized that while we both use computers and technology all day, business team members largely glide through their days without ever having exposure to computer-specific language like "No Sync Input." The whole business side of an organization (The Business) spends time doing business and not digging into how it uses technology.

My colleague and his fellow team members drive the organization's productivity regardless of what platform or code underlies it all. We never consider unique perspectives. It's akin to taking your smartphone apart before making a call—something we'd never do. That said, it's a good reminder of how beneficial it can be to help colleagues in another part of the organization. People get good at what they do, but that doesn't always include knowledge of optimizing, troubleshooting, or fixing things about the tools used for the task. My colleague, puzzled by the "No Sync Input" problem, was a finance expert yet not skilled at fixing technology, and that's by organizational design—fitting within duties and responsibilities.

While collaboration methods exist to bridge the gap, some relationship aspects may still need to be noticed. Evaluating individuals solely on role performance might miss the bigger picture. Inherent contrasts persist across organizational shifts, tactical team structures, and innovative service models, integrating solutions from diverse perspectives across the organization. To remain conscious of the divide and factor in leadership expectations, I've coined "the thin wide line."

The Limited "Thin" Perspective

- When forming a project team, the thin leadership expectation, rightly so, is a simplistic line in the sand on which team members can easily traverse back and forth. Organized as tactical collaboration, leaders assign team members to collaborate.

The Comprehensive "Wide" Perspective

- In contrast to the "thin" perspective, a more grounded viewpoint acknowledges and appreciates the diversity among team members. The "wide" represents the need to catalyze a transformative movement. This happens when technical developers do not understand the tasks they are redeveloping, and business team members know nothing of what new technology is capable of. From the "wide" perspective, imagining and building a realistic future becomes tremendously challenging.

Abundant Reasons for Disconnect

Performance along the "thin wide line" is more intriguing than the divergent perspectives included. Under executive leadership, team members are brought together into a neatly ordered organization of groups and teams with a focused scope that supports and responds to shifts in management and management thinking from above. Proactive project managers and line of business leaders lead tactical teams with a streamlined approach that supports organizational aspirations.

During execution, business team members drive productivity and handle all business tasks, while technical team members provide support. Managers work hard to bridge that gap, but ultimately, communicating and delegating tasks and time effectively without accounting for differences in behavior will cause disappointment. At some point, the implicit expectation is to go the extra mile, invest time in what others do, and get a fuller understanding of the flow in the extended ecosystem. It can seem time-consuming and occasionally short-term use when needed most, but it is critical. For example, if business teams need to collect information, the immediate tech response will be data collection by creating a form. Beyond essential use, look at the differences in behavior between these two individuals: a developer building a form and one from the business using it. A simple comparison sheds light on the difference.

The Technical Team Member

- Invest in development, coding, layout, and form flow verification hours.
- Scopes work effort in terms of development hours.
- Any hours not dedicated to development result in compromised functionality.

The Business Team Member

- Requires minutes to complete, submit, and move on.
- Specifies requirements based on a segment of the workflow.
- Experiences considerable frustration with even seconds of delay.

The final point for both highlights the issue's core, and, unsurprisingly, both the developer and the business team members experience similar frustration. Sharing the common obstacle of needing help to complete their primary tasks, there is a significant disconnect in how the problem is perceived and addressed. The developer's focus on refining the technical aspects clashes with the business team's urgent need for productivity and task completion. Misalignment creates a tension between the pursuit of perfection and the demand for timely results, hindering overall progress.

Beyond the Thin and the Wide

Traditionally, organizational roles have been based on discrete skill sets, and the modern business landscape continues to evolve into a very different beast. Success in such a fluid, fast-paced ecosystem depends on team members' ability to move beyond traditional roles as technical or business professionals and adopt a more generalist role, at least in a core set of skills to support the organization. While specific areas of expertise are crucial, team members must also understand the tactical tools and processes that power the organization.

As celebratory interactions, organizations should mandate cross-functional employee training programs to foster a more comprehensive understanding. Programs could provide foundational knowledge of business strategies, methodologies, and the overall operational landscape of the company. By equipping all team members with shared knowledge, the organization can break down silos, enhance collaboration, and work toward the same goals.

Furthermore, leadership should pay particular attention to unique translators who can speak the languages of business stakeholders and technology folks. As unicorns of your organization, they engage with cable swingers and tech nerds, converting complex technical concepts into simple business insights in the blink of an eye. They also facilitate communication and understanding with the business, so AI initiatives use the best technical capabilities to achieve overarching business objectives.

Acknowledging and recognizing unique organizational translators fosters a culture of knowledge-sharing and understanding, where team members are inspired to push past the "thin wide line." It's not enough to focus only on an area of responsibility; as lines blend and blur with artificial intelligence, team members need a global perspective on how they support the organization's mission.

Organizational Synchronization and Harmony

Aligned correctly and driving productivity, organizations can make beautiful music. Most likely, it's not the best sound, but regardless, it's a symphony of productivity—that seamless flow of individuals crushing tasks, rolling up metrics, breaking the last high. Much like a shareholder utopia, team members know their roles, are proactive and motivated, and drive forward with value-pushing organizational goals.

While perfect synchronization is ideal, most organizations don't measure up. Imagine the organization driving together on a coffee run, with each team member controlling one element of the vehicle—steering, brakes, gas, and so on. Fragmented and inefficient, complexity escalates as the organization grows. Maintaining alignment amidst change is difficult and fuels fears of job losses, especially concerning artificial intelligence.

Collaboration and workflow optimization will naturally uncover opportunities for transformative AI implementation. Alignment is needed before, during, and after every transformation to empower the organization and its people to evolve and thrive continuously. The following core alignment strategies foster internal synchronization, creating a sense of security and readiness for the future.

Culture of Intelligence

Embracing a "culture of intelligence" promotes thoughtful decision making to strengthen organizational performance and drives appreciation for diverse opinions. Identifying and improving behaviors rooted in traditional "just how we do things" business processes (e.g., strict regulation, overly rigid, inflexible) can be an initial celebration of the commitment to evolve.

Even the most straightforward process, when reviewed with a group of team members who are directly involved and those who are not, raises awareness and significantly helps develop professional competencies. I'm reminded of a workflow discussion during one of many roadmap workshops, where one team member described emailing a spreadsheet to another team member at the organization. To everyone's amazement, even after executing this process for years and working in the same building, these two people had never met in person!

A significant oversight, the lack of interaction, reveals that effective interaction is a cultural challenge within the organization. Having the correct data, tools, and supportive face-to-face interaction fosters a culture where knowledge grows, and everyone can leverage information effectively, reinforcing the need for team members to become better business and technical translators to get past the "thin, wide line."

There is a significant gap to overcome; some will be better than others and may maintain focus on one side or the other; it's now a requirement that everyone in the organization become proficient "business and technical translators," capable of understanding the needs of both business and technical teams. This entails comprehending business objectives, requirements, and technical limitations and effectively communicating across these domains. It also necessitates active listening and empathy to foster shared understanding. Moreover, bridging the gap between data and action is essential, meaning analyzing data and leveraging insights to guide decision making, strategy, and innovation. By cultivating a "translator" mindset, organizations can create a more collaborative and informed culture, enabling better use of data and ultimately leading to improved business outcomes.

Collaborative and Continuous Improvement

A culture of intelligence never ends, accepting good ideas from anyone at any time. That said, it may not be surprising that the organization, in support of building a culture of intelligence, should also support a culture of association, creating opportunities for effective teamwork, learning, and development. By doing so, organizations work together through interactive sessions grounded in engagement, from one-on-one discussions to organizational perspectives. The distinction between reactive feedback and proactive improvement can be seen in shifting the question of "what did we mess up" to proclaiming that "tomorrow we will do better."

Success Through Adaptation

An organization's ability to navigate its internal landscape is critical to achieving remarkable success. Organizations can nourish adaptation by sharing stories of everyday successes, both in the form of successful paths taken and failures representing paths not taken. "Accepting trial and error means accepting error. It means taking problems in stride when plans don't work out, which is not something human brains seem able to do without a struggle."[12] As a simple practice, celebrating the paths not taken with the corresponding success helps foster a culture of collective achievement and strengthens bonds within the workforce.

Highlighting the impact of individual efforts promotes camaraderie and provides employees with a sense of identity and value. To sustain change, regularly evaluate progress. Instead of dwelling on failures and complexity, focus on course corrections—furthermore, individual and organizational transitions, particularly regarding analytical maturity alignment. Pinpoint areas for improvement and make necessary adjustments along the way.

Cross-Functional Performance

The tendency of workgroups to focus exclusively on individual metrics without considering broader organizational context has always puzzled me. It's akin to evaluating the productivity of a lemonade stand solely by the number of cups made, without factoring in crucial elements like supplies or sales. A narrow focus leads to unrealistic expectations. A lack of connectivity to the organization ignores the proper drivers of success, even more significantly if employees' compensation is misaligned. If productivity is hindered due to limited resources or staffing challenges, like a team member being on vacation or extended leave, expecting the metrics to remain unaffected is impractical and counterproductive. It creates undue pressure on individuals and disregards the interconnectedness of various organizational elements.

In the spirit of flowing water, from source to sink, individual performance can be evaluated through an expansion within the framework of the larger organizational ecosystem. Factors such as resource availability, team dynamics, and external influences can all be considered. By understanding how elements impact individual and team performance, organizations can set more realistic expectations, identify bottlenecks, and provide targeted support, ultimately leading to sustainable growth and success.

Cross-functional performance evaluation helps everyone consider extended ideas to solve problems, providing communal analysis and evaluation. In other words, it fosters a culture of success, creating an organizational rhythm that can unlock broader cross-sharing performance. A "rhythm" that seeks opportunities to replace manual segments with intelligent machines.

In organizational collaborations, it is essential to consider team support versus individual underperformance: acknowledgment and a brief intermission to recenter and create a responsible space to foster mutual support among groups. The errors become shared rather than one person doing something wrong. Through disciplined, strategic implementations, we can reward individuals for cooperating in analyses that enhance their managerial success. Here are a few approaches to help foster growth:

Connect: Assign liaisons to interface between departments and groups, bridge communities, and translate information and teamwork on analytics initiatives. By amalgamating elements across the organization, liaisons dissolve silos and motivate systemic problem-solving, ensuring efforts align with overarching goals. They also help drive informal connections by knowing who can help with what is needed across the organization.

Experiment: Assemble cross-functional teams with diverse expertise for early white-box testing to solve intricate issues requiring an interdisciplinary approach. Members leverage collective knowledge, gaining insights from others while imparting new skills, culminating in ingenious solutions. They then return to share insights and interactions with respective teams.

Show them the money: Institute incentive structures focused on impactful alignment, including bonuses, promotions, recognition programs, and professional growth opportunities. These structures further spawn virtuous cycles where teamwork value is reinforced and desired working relationships are endogenously maintained among colleagues.

Go beyond references and guides: Build standardized, consistent, and repeatable frameworks to guide conduct. A centralized workspace should house references, procedures, analysis, and insights. Encourage discussion and debate, furthering a perpetual betterment and progress culture.

Take the time to mentor: Mentorship programs effectively pair veterans with those who could benefit from the experience. Mentors provide counsel, facilitate knowledge transfer, aid emerging analytical talent for the future, and, even more significantly, find community. Every organization is different, but if aligned and applied correctly to support AI, these activities promote an environment where, as Alison Wilson says, "Data science is a team sport. As data grows in volume, velocity, variety, and veracity, solving complex problems can't be done in a silo."[13] Efforts will result in better decision making, enhanced creativity, and a high level of triumph for both individuality and entity.

Productivity is naturally boosted by directly acknowledging contributions. Breaking organizational aims into granular performance markers attuned to individual influence encourages a collaborative spirit by emphasizing personal stakes in the company's continued well-being. Allowing teammates to candidly celebrate triumphs in authentic voices, such as "I helped make this happen," is profoundly motivating. It stands apart from customary leadership addresses where plaudits are offered broadly, with executives providing credit through pronouncements like "You all made this happen." It's an adjusted viewpoint that validates and festoons individual efforts, nurturing a sense of possession and delight. When the workforce feels labor immediately impacts corporate prosperity, morale swells, involvement intensifies, and inspiration grows. In the same positive spirit, the same authentic voice can confidently declare, "This is not our path," and celebrate failures as successes—recognizing individuals' efforts to explore less fruitful directions. When honest efforts and authentic ownership support learning, growth accelerates exponentially. Moreover, such a philosophy fosters a culture of transparency and liability. It redirects the narrative from a top-down approach to a more collaborative one, where all voices and inputs are valued. Ultimately, empowering individuals to claim their role in the organization's success cultivates a sense of shared duty and collective purpose, driving greater participation and improved consequences.

Leadership and Strategic Alignment

The quality and dedication of an organization's leadership determine the effectiveness of inspiration and guidance in supporting shared goals.

Leaders must act according to the organization's values, provide clear direction, and focus on developing analytical skills across the workforce.

Influential leaders create a continuous cycle of reflection and action that fosters self-motivated responsibility and clarity of purpose within their teams, empowering them to take initiative and contribute to organizational success. They also ensure team members own the work, remain accountable, and receive recognition, resulting in higher engagement and output. Not to mention, corresponding burnout rates are also further reduced.[14]

Recognizing and Celebrating Harmony

As alignment strategies highlight, fostering open communication and in-person knowledge-sharing is crucial for coordinated action. Interactive and in-person approaches establish a harmonious balance between individual and organizational analytical maturity, ensuring that high-performing analysts are positioned to maximize their impact, share their perspectives, and ultimately up-level the team. Research shows organizational socialization boosts team innovation through employee voice, especially with supportive leadership. Furthermore, it highlights the value of interactive, in-person meetings to foster connections and encourage open communication, ultimately driving innovation.[15] Integrating modern tools and technologies into managerial processes is a critical missing element in support of extended organizational alignment, as they provide the means to effectively track and celebrate managerial harmony, fostering a culture of collaboration and continuous improvement.

Internal Alignment: A Harmonious Approach

Decisions made within a company have a ripple effect that extends far beyond boardrooms and strategic plans. Even a simple yes or no in the boardroom can influence how external audiences behave, an impact that should be noticed. Focusing solely on internal needs, even if it seems good for the organization, can make it harder to understand your audience. Internal change leading to an external adjustment should be treated cautiously. Disrupting pricing, product features, or how your audience interacts with your brand can surprise and diminish their loyalty.

Consider an organization under cost pressure to raise prices or restructure pricing (from user-based to consumption pricing, for example). While the decision might seem essential to get the house in order, it could also create a backlash among customers who can't justify the cost adequately with a new structure and become upset that they're not being heard anymore. When that happens, the floodgates open, and a mass exodus follows—at this point, it is all hands on deck to salvage anything from the crumbling foundation. Regrettably, the damage is already done; you've significantly changed your audience's behavior. By shifting to a usage-based pricing model, you've inadvertently sent a message to your customers: everything they do comes with a cost. It's akin to entering an arcade with limited funds; you'll only engage with the most essential activities, and the likelihood of returning significantly diminishes.

Organizations must strengthen the connection between internal execution and external experiences, providing transparent communication about internal decisions' impact on their audience. In today's world, loyalty takes time to build. When organizations successfully balance internal operations with external offerings, they create a fluid environment to foster lasting relationships.

Exponential Flow in Organizational Operations

The organization's team is deployed daily to push the vision forward, get everything done, and achieve goals! In doing so, leaders hope every team member will be imbued with universal organizational situational awareness and adaptability. Like being the sole driver of your organization's productivity vehicle, desirable as it may sound, it's most likely out of bounds and unattainable.

Growth, often triggered by external factors or internal catalysts (like individual actions), truly accelerates when personal decisions align with broader productivity goals. Publicly traded companies and even

Figure 2.4 The rotary paradox: A visual metaphor for unmanaged flow

startups experience growth cycles and are subject to scalable expansion models. Although many have solved reporting and work distribution issues, an end-to-end organizational framework that tracks the organization's development and behavioral traits is generally lacking. Similarly, fluid evolution requires operational oversight, optimization, and process improvement. It begins from an immutable foundation with distinct mechanisms for defining workflows (e.g., jobs), managing them cleanly, and governing the workflow life cycle. Be mindful of the nature of organizational processes, especially unmanaged self-sustaining processes: they look good on the surface but can lead to severe problems. It's like a rotary: by relying on individual decisions, it keeps traffic moving but doesn't allow overall flow control, leading to congestions, accidents, and other issues (Figure 2.4).

Effective communication is scarce during organizational restructuring. Due to changes, work assignments and workflows are suddenly altered when they are not adequately analyzed (or where no documentation exists). Even though the layout looks better on paper, it may not improve the overall effectiveness or pageantry long after the shift.

As minor alterations in an ecosystem can have cascading effects, minor organizational changes also impact functioning and human constituents.

Nonrecorded organizational change and misalignments result in confusion, ambiguity, and inefficiency in operations; consequently, an organization becomes less agile, adaptive, and dynamic. When documenting workflows and change processes, it is important to focus on alignment. This means tracking and measuring all activities to ensure the organization achieves its overall goals.

Why so much attention to organizational flow? Influence depends on sequencing, so it's only possible to strategically incorporate influence to achieve desired outcomes by effectively managing an organization's processes, operations, and corresponding interactions. Expanding organizational workflow mapping should include, but not be limited to the following:

Documenting changes (meticulous record-keeping):

- Maintain a comprehensive and detailed record of all changes to organizational structures, workflows, and processes. This record, a treasure chest of historical data, provides reference points for comprehending the impact of past decisions on operations, facilitating informed decision making for the future. We often remember decisions, especially when they are highly polarized, but need more supporting context to stand back and understand the whole picture.

Assessing impact (proactive analysis):

- Impact assessments are essential, and leaders should consider potential consequences in various business areas before implementing changes. As a proactive approach, impact assessments reassure organizations about the effectiveness of the decision-making process, allowing them to anticipate and mitigate potential challenges.

Communicating (transparent information sharing

- Effective communication is vital during organizational change. All stakeholders should be informed about the changes, rationale, and expected outcomes. Transparent communication ensures all members feel included and informed, fostering understanding and acceptance and facilitating a smoother transition.

Monitor and evaluate (continuous improvement):

- Implementing changes is not a one-time event; it's an ongoing process. Continuous monitoring and evaluation of the impact of changes enable organizations to identify areas for improvement and make necessary adjustments. It promotes agility and responsiveness as a feedback loop, allowing the organization to adapt to evolving needs and challenges.

Adopting broader organizational mapping combined with a data-driven approach to change management is how organizations move toward constant improvement, maximizing operations' benefits. Above all, it's a preventive measure that exposes and avoids accidental restructuring and promotes agility.

Combining a fluid organizational structure with extended information distribution produces synergy, introducing opportunities for robust cross-department solutions that drive transformative changes and infinite progression. When operations and analytics are synchronized, a new level of decision making emerges, leading to more informed decisions relevant to future trends and enabling proactive problem-solving and innovation. Business intelligence (BI) systems should make data easily accessible across the operational structure, aligning it with each workgroup and providing overall organizational metrics for each unit. However, many BI systems do not do this automatically as it encourages users to continue using their platform and purchase more licenses.

Exponential Operational Management

As scary as exponential growth can seem to manage for leadership and team members, there's no fear of it in the investor's wallet. An enormous part of the workforce is merely there to shield against gargantuan growth spikes and cope with problems brought about by such fast scaling. Nevertheless, having work itemized and understanding how information or tasks flow within the institution is crucial.

Zoom out and imagine your organization as a massive lazy river, gently carrying tasks and teams … and delivering them all too easily, refreshing relaxation. The need for active task management? Your audience flows around in their "tube" as a product or service, but what is being navigated on this river will differ for employees.

Like a leisurely float down the lazy river, there might be unexpected logjams of inflatable flamingos or a surprise waterfall around the bend. Regardless, the current carries everyone along; in the same manner, the organization keeps progressing despite unforeseen detours and challenges.

The lazy river is a rough analogy but nicely illustrates that you must understand your organization's flow and the roles team members can play to help with it.

Overloading the workforce with too much work or unrealistic expectations can lead to chaos, burnout, and low productivity. In the long run, it keeps the organization from reaching its goals. Achieving the right balance of progress and workload, stability brightens the mood, and a stable organization comes with understanding your organizational flow, a direct line to what each employee contributes, and a proper expectation of what each team member can do. All things that are required well before employing an artificial machineforce. Prepare your ecosystem, then embrace the power of AI.

Sustain the Flow in an AI-Driven World

Evaluating growth potential often leads to extensive reflection about the level of focus and commitment to sustain continuous, exponential growth. Startups aiming for public status face the challenge of maintaining consistent quarter-over-quarter and year-over-year growth while navigating internal development. Revenue growth stems from a steady flow driven by external and internal demand and effective demand-generation strategies.

As perfect as exponential growth may seem, at least in the shareholder's eyes, the organization lacks comprehensive frameworks supporting tactical process refinement. Beyond mere decisions, there's an extensive need for oversight, alignment, optimization, and transformation—and it's not just more management or replacing processes with new technology. Such a framework would systematically define, integrate, manage, and govern organizational workflows. It would provide transparency into human and machine interactions within and beyond the organizational structure, preserve historical data, and generate scenarios for the future. When adopting new technology, evidence from the comprehensive framework would fundamentally change workflows and reduce management overhead.

Furthermore, synchronizing operational and analytical components is essential for AI to participate effectively in the organization's missions. As a ground-truthing synergy, these two, in collaboration, can support transforming business processes, unlocking cross-organizational solutions, and driving organizational evolution. A cohesive interplay between operations and analytics fosters informed decision making and strategic planning, enhancing accuracy, insights, and adaptability.

Go Beyond Conventional "Use Cases"

Throughout my multidecade career, one standard question has resounded through countless meetings, conference calls, and conference halls. Often an easy icebreaker but typically over-relied on by parties looking for a shortcut, it's expressively delivered; "What's the use case?"

Depending on the inquiry, this simple four-word question often demands some prefabricated response or—in its more antagonistic forms—a passive-aggressive way of testing knowledge. On the surface, it appears to be a simple ask, but underneath lies an assumption that underlines so much of what we are told should make up our lives or matter. It is a sign that people want to see real things and gain material from concrete ideas or technology before spending time or resources on it. The fact that everybody is after "use cases" can sometimes drive innovation but also understandably makes it harder to explore something completely new without the push for immediate commercialization.

The "use case" (or, more appropriately, "you case") question should ideally serve as a vector directing our attention toward problems, but it is also downright misguided. It takes the summation of iteration, effort, and process to assume it is neatly packaged instead of understanding the complicated and distributed splatter that constitutes an area of interest (AOI). Work in the real world is not linear but varied, requiring adaptations to all types of people, processes, and things happening. To push beyond the "you case"-focused world and get at true innovation (not only about digitization or automation, as everyone seems to believe), I have continuously and intentionally reframed conversations around "AOIs." A slight change effectively expands human boundaries set forth by use cases, leading to a broader and more strategic workflow mindset.

Even as team members grapple with messy real-world factors that tend to hinder our romantic use cases, the AOI promotes an inclusive discussion—an expansive user-centered exploration instead of a straitjacket. AOIs are not a replacement for use case efforts as the organization needs both mindsets: one focused on the use case and another AOI-focused, each with its own merits and demerits from a problem-solving perspective. Embracing both and framing discussions around an AOI allows the entire team to understand the expanded context and provide situational support. A simple way to educate the team: the region of your interest (AOI) may have multiple use cases, and some of those use cases will be contextual permutations (other perspectives) of one-use case. As we plow forward with artificial intelligence, illuminating and comparing the organization's flow at the AOI level will provide extensive alignment with the use cases of intelligent machines. Here's a deeper comparison for further understanding.

The ""*Use Case*"" Mindset

Focus: Narrowly scoped, typically addressing a specific task or scenario from the perspective of a single user or role. While providing clarity and precision, this approach risks overlooking broader implications and opportunities for flow optimization.

Benefits: It targets a clear pain point for rapid wins and improvements. Implementation and measurement are simplified when the domain is constrained. However, such a myopic lens may need to pay more attention to profound systemic flaws or miss opportunities for holistic, innovative solutions.

Limitations: Use cases developed in a vacuum can be disjointed and often fail to consider extended workflow. Quick fixes treat symptoms, not root causes, and problems may persist or reemerge elsewhere. Significant opportunities for advancing the broader mission may be passed over.

Example: Optimizing a specific checkout interaction in isolation, though useful, provides little insight into customer journeys end-to-end and how procurement might be re-engineered for an improved experience overall.

The ""*Area of Interest*"" Mindset

Focus: Encompassing multiple interconnected aspects within a broader context, AOIs seek to represent interdependent use cases as they interact throughout organizational processes and systems, providing an opportunity to craft influential upstream interventions and optimize complex journeys.

Benefits: Framing AOIs allows all participants to speak their understanding, provides investigative freedom, seeks a holistic perspective, and cultivates a deep understanding of challenges or potential across boundaries. Identifying and addressing the root causes promises sustainable progress via systemic redesign. Innovation thrives where comprehensive visions are pursued.

Limitations: Ambitious scope demands cross-team cooperation and long-term alignment. Comprehensive solutions are challenging to

implement at scale immediately, and tangible benefits material-
ize slower as changes percolate through interlocking functions.
Hitting this limitation may require a use case fix to bring together
an AOI.

Example: Re-engineering procurement, delivery, and customer
service touch-points as an integrated supply chain aims to vastly
improve experience, though short-term wins still need to be
achieved during such disruptive transformation.

While increasingly focused on applications is prudent depending on
circumstances, disregarding a broader view when addressing explicit
objectives constrains organizational evolution. Sometimes, a targeted
tactic is preferable; other times, a more encompassing perspective is
needed.

Examining AOIs permits examining solitary tasks, including
overarching domains and how diverse functions interact. It's not only a
method to open discussions but is pivotal for incorporating AI, allowing
preliminary and subsequent functionalities to be customized for a
smoother workflow. AOIs highlight procedure inefficiencies, culminating in balanced productivity and an improved working experience.
Understanding the merits and constraints of individual mindsets aids in
determining the most effective approach. Frequently blending viewpoints achieves the best outcome. The root causes or potentials are
examined comprehensively, and solutions are separated into workable
applications.

Historically, use cases offered a shared framework for comprehension and collaboration, surmounting technology adoption challenges.
However, with AI's abilities expanding beyond simple use cases, this
old-school rigid framework needs to be revised. Altering terminology
is significant, but it also affects how we discuss topics. Discussion
frameworks centered around AOIs can transform our understanding
and collaboration, moving from isolated use cases to holistic journeys
and aiding teams in grasping modern work's complex information flows,
decision making, and actions.

Active Engagement Discussion Frameworks

It's such a waste, the loss of time in meetings when our thoughts drift. Critical information often gets lost or undiscussed in a struggling conversation, and engagement falls further as time passes. Inevitably, this results in another "follow-up" meeting that goes over the same discussions and must make decisions we should have made when all is fresh. As much as I feel an agenda is mandatory when requesting time, so should be the expected discussion type. I'm also sure the meeting-centric nature of modern employment has somewhat ruined the desire to be prepared ahead of time; it echoes in questioning attendance.

Is preparation required or just participation? Will I be actively involved, or should I expect my attendance to be enough if my chair is full?

Too often, gatherings prioritize attendance over quality content and respect for everyone's time. It's time to transform our approach and focus on meaningful and structured events as we embrace connection. It's time to think differently, especially as we integrate AI into our organizations. We must create spaces beyond physical locations that foster diverse perspectives and meaningful conversations by developing standardized frameworks to guide the discussion. Ones that convert any unruly, preach-to-the-choir meeting into an easily digested visual aid for prompt assembly action.

Discussion frameworks have proven their magic as a mindset-shifting practice throughout my multidecade tenure. Problems are complex and vary for each organization, but customizable "OneSheets" help align AOIs into one collective voice. Instead of shallow talking, personal soap boxes, or self-focused monologuing, one piece of paper adequately organized can drive extensive progress and understanding. More importantly, standardized and repeatable discussion frameworks are the most effective means of aligning an organization's business and technical sides and, in effect, tackling the "thin wide line."

Meaningless meetings are replaced by meaningful collaboration around outcomes. Eventually, these structured processes become second nature to the teams after early repetition, leading to more efficiency and unity. The expertise also extends to external collaborations, fostering client confidence and enhancing returns.

When an organization has regard for both aspects (collaboration and excellence), disruptive frameworks are reignited by the influence architect to drive seamless synergy between internal and external touch points throughout business interactions of various types within your company.

Crafting Discussion Frameworks

As powerful tools to guide conversations, discussion frameworks produce productive outcomes and better alignment with critical objectives while, at the same time, developing standardized and repeatable behavior across the organization. The "one sheet" concept also forces detachment from the natural entertainment of interactive technology and hits at the heart of human recollection. The act of writing things down, even on a whiteboard, has a profound impact on the audience, reinforcing ideas and demonstrating attentiveness. To maximize their effectiveness, adhere to these guiding principles.

Brevity and one-sheet focus:

- As a starting point, develop the contents on one sheet of paper; the front should have your main story, whereas the back could hold a teaser or other supporting information. From a concise focus, it's possible to scale the discussion to other mediums like presentation slides, whiteboards, and so on. Illustrations and graphics are necessary to explain content better and position the context. Visual information is the easiest and most efficient way to describe a big concept or make this structure more engaging. Your audience may not remember everything you say, but they will remember the visuals and key off them.

Provocative questions and contextual cues:

- The front of the sheet offers an opportunity to ask three or fewer provocative, high-level questions that challenge participants' thinking and encourage a deeper examination of the subject matter. Provide an overview with some background before delving into questioning. For example, include visuals to help explain the intent of each question.

Interactive, inclusive, and repetitive:

- Plan to be interactive. Close laptops and turn off phones. The framework should allow participants to write, draw, and share thoughts. Illustrations provide visual communication and inspire interaction, leading to further participation and accountability in conversation. Invite members to draw on the paper ... circle relevant images, cross out irrelevant ones ..., and sketch examples. Doing so will help everyone visually see how each team member thinks!

Consistency, reproducibility, and portability:

- Ensure your base framework is a standard template for discussion, providing consistency and ease of use throughout teams or projects. The framework should fit groups of various sizes and skill levels.

Audience-centric and collaborative:

- Adjust your frameworks based on what works for your audience's level of understanding. Consider demographics, motivations, and potential objections. The audience must be able to use the sheet independently after two or three walkthroughs.

Iterative process:

- Open your frameworks to user experience and outcomes-based feedback. Always look to iterate and deliver the best results with your approach. Allow for an open environment where everyone feels encouraged to voice their mind and express themselves as a ladder.

A cohesive one-sheet framework nurtures alignment and authenticity at a deeper level, encouraging teams to tap into collective intelligence. As such practices are implemented with understanding, they become sturdy platforms for commutative imagination, scholarly criticism, and synergic decision making. The one-sheet framework offers a malleable, structured space for intermingling ideas and approaches to spark new insights, and it's why they are still such practical tools for quick exchanges and easy memorization. They even act as a physical grounding, helping keep everyone *on the same page* during discussions and making it convenient to retrace essential tidbits.

In essence, one-sheet discussion frameworks are intended to be a bridge between individual minds for unleashing shared potential. They create a shared context that reshapes knowledge not as transmitted but as produced. The shared context leads to greater comprehension, leading to more reasoned decisions. Ultimately, one-sheet discussion frameworks result in greater social convergence.

Transforming Obstacles: Bridging the Divide

A few years ago, an impressionable meeting with a multinational bank's senior management further demonstrated the difficulty in effective communication and collaboration. Our team, an AI platform vendor, could not connect with the executives the way we had planned, and instead of having interested leadership, we had somewhat disgruntled executives. It was functional, but our industry VP, a colleague of the executives, focused on being polite and fantastic success stories. While the stories resonated, someone else's success evoked an all-too-common response: "That's not how we do things." Still puzzled, the clock was ticking. Hearing "I don't understand what you do" from the same executive three times was almost a death knell. Thankfully, our account manager resorted to a last-hope effort—one that, under the guidance of our VP industry expert, wasn't a good interaction for such an influential audience. Introducing our OneSheet discussion framework for the path to successful AI, the team now held a visual guide—a simple single-page document with three questions and graphics to guide our conversation.

1. *Where to start?*
2. *How would this help?*
3. *Frame a predictive question!*

It took less than zero minutes to change the conversation, recasting our product in a light that made sense to the executives. It was visually engaging and provided an easy-to-reference structure that helped reduce confusion and ensure everyone was on a similar page. Finally, it allowed us to capture the client's journey, as opposed to sharing others' success, and in doing so, highlight how our achievements supported their context.

Last-minute success taught us the importance of an AOI-focused, structured method to explain our actions. Helping everyone understand the processing and organizational flow with interrelated activity streams also underscored linking organizational goals with AI's supporting decision science.

Often overlooked or set aside in the interest of time, we must build an integrated workplace where every force, humans and machines, knows the efforts behind the scenes and how they, as individuals, contribute to the organization. A discussion framework guides different perspectives forward in alignment, encouraging the exchange of ideas, creating a connected environment, and celebrating wins at all levels. Invest in, respect, and empower your organizational forces, human and machine.

The Power of Diverse Perspectives

Thinking beyond individual use cases is essential for teams to truly grasp the interconnectedness of today's and, more importantly, tomorrow's business functions. Analogies and storytelling can inspire and bridge the gap, making complex concepts relatable and fostering a deeper understanding of how the various parts of an organization fit together.

Using effective discussion frameworks combined with storytelling, we can share experiences, lessons learned, and insights about the overall journey. A joint vision, from multiple perspectives—ones that run different parts of the organization—creates a shared understanding and aligns everyone toward achieving the overarching goals. Remember, our organizational roles shape our experience, offering a unique but limited view of the whole picture. As distinct perspectives, these workforce "vantage points" are invaluable in uncovering hidden insights and realizing an organization's full potential. Each point, whether from an individual, a department, or a team, provides a valuable piece of the puzzle and, when shared, helps to foster better collaboration and optimize organizational flow by appreciating and integrating these diverse viewpoints.

By embracing a holistic approach that combines exploring AOIs with diverse viewpoints, we can identify and seize opportunities, optimize processes, and build a shared vision for the future. Going beyond surface-level analysis, we can uncover underlying factors to drive organizational success. Your organization's data is a vast ocean teeming with potential insights that are unlocked from the team's unique perspectives and vantage points. Navigating effectively requires casting with experience and extensive awareness, remembering these concepts:

> Net size significance: Just as the size and mesh of a fishing net determine what is caught, the scope and granularity of your data collection methods must align with your vantage point. Misaligned methods can lead to misleading or incomplete conclusions.
>
> Depth of exploration: The ocean's depths hold hidden treasures. Similarly, deeper dives into your data can reveal intricate insights. Still, much like the extensiveness of the great abyss, it requires focused effort and patience and may not result in any findings.

Net type, span, and mesh size: The methods you use to gather data (scanning, concentrated inquiry, and so on) and the breadth of your data collection matter. A wider net will capture more information but demands more attention and analysis.

Ultimately, like a skilled sailor navigating the ocean, understanding your data and its vantage points is about extracting the specific insights you need to steer your organization toward success.

Embracing Change and Adaptability

As tempting as it is to look at what we do well—the standard stuff—that shortsighted perspective restricts us from achieving more and seeing the forest for all those trees (even if it's a kelp forest in our ocean of data). While predictive analytics can offer shades of gray, machine learning only predicts! We humans interpret predictions as guidance to make decisions.

If a model predicts a customer will likely churn, we don't immediately pick up the phone and call the customers to say we know they are leaving! We must step back and understand why, determine how best to fix the problem, and not make it creepily worse. Excellent decision making goes beyond the data, considering the larger AOI, with all its vantage points and perspectives as options for influential interactions.

The organization evolves, and workflows change; stay aware of micro-level shifts—zoom in and out to understand the viewpoint at all levels. Automation will excel in certain areas, while human flexibility remains crucial in others. If it's hard to visualize, consider your organization a lazy river, flowing with currents moving at different paces and sometimes in opposing directions. Understanding dynamics allows you to leverage AI and navigate the complexities more effectively and strategically. Here are some other ways to look at the flows of your organization.

Enjoying calm waters?

- Steady, predictable work gets done within your organization. Consider repetitive work, easily defined processes, and set working methods. AI automation can thrive in these smooth waters, picking routine tasks by the computer system and letting human resources concentrate on more important tasks, improving overall efficiency.

Experiencing turbulent rapids?

- Your organization's quick-moving, ever-changing parts require innovation and reading the room. This category includes new product development, market research, and customer engagement initiatives. While AI can deliver great insights and predictions, human judgment, creativity, and long-term strategic thinking still have to row across this river.

Missing hidden undercurrents?

- Hidden influences or risks below the surface may not be on bright display but have an incredible impact on your organization. Undercurrents can include employee morale, potential supply chain disruptions, or emerging competitor threats. AI can identify and keep track of these undercurrents, enabling preemptive risk mitigation and providing a roadmap for strategic responses.

Stuck in whirlpools?

- Representing the whirlpools in your organization, they can range from departmental silos and poor communication to general (human) resistance to change. With AI-powered analytics, organizations can gain valuable insights into the causal factors of these problems, ultimately providing conflict resolution and nurturing a better work environment in unity.

Too many eddys?

- Financial reporting, payroll, and inventory management are examples of processes that cycle consistently in your organization. Although these may be mundane processes, they are crucial to the functioning of your service. The eddies will work well with AI automation, making them consistent, accurate, and fast.

Looming countercurrents?

• These are more difficult to identify in a time of constant transition but "come from opposing pressures at work within the organization. If left unaddressed, they can form hurdles and stand in the way. By analyzing employee sentiment, customer feedback, or market trends, AI can pick up these countercurrents, allowing you to recognize and resolve conflicts before they blow up."

Stuck in turbulent flow?

• Turbulent flow includes periods of unstable/chaotic nature, which can be due to internal conflicts, external pull/push forces from the market, or sudden events. Turbulent flow requires adaptability and resilience. Using AI, real-time insights and predictive analytics are possible, which can help you sail through turbulence with informed decision making during uncertainty.

As you learn to read diverse currents within the organization and purposefully apply AI initiatives, you can tap into immense potential, tackle obstacles, and capitalize on opportunities. Remember, the flow will constantly evolve, and the ability to adapt and use AI-informed insights is critical if you want ongoing success. Regularly observing these "currents" within your organization allows for informed decisions, better navigation of challenges, and proactive steering toward your goals.

Exponential Everything

Traditional staffing models hardly promise an ×2 or ×5 growth, even if optimal in terms of efficiency, and technology adds extra complexity, requiring even more talent. AOIs within and across organizations must be nurtured, expanded, and aligned to goals proactively supporting growth. As with any exponential trajectory, careful management is necessary. As such, remember that rocket-powered acceleration merely marks the very beginning of the journey. For teams focused on day-to-day activities, exponential change is extremely daunting; hence, there is a need to negotiate and deal with the mental impact of drastic change. More than individual mindsets, the future needs minds (and machines) interconnected across organizational boundaries. At the same time, teamwork in and of itself is not exactly a novel concept. The need for a shared vision across this cross-functional team is critical to making this approach actionable. Not only does anticipation nurture collaboration, but the sky is the limit with holding on to integration, release, or joint venture objectives in long-term partnerships. Align your workforce, machineforce, goals, and influence to embrace an exponential future.

CHAPTER 3

Elevating Organizational Intelligence

The most mature don't always act like it and may be unaware of it.

Organizational intelligence is an overwhelming concept involving many aspects and complexities. As an entrepreneur and organizational leader, you have a vision, but how to implement it, what will motivate your team, and how to ensure they thrive involves more than technical knowledge with good intentions or just financial capital. Organizational intelligence creates an atmosphere where people are motivated and developing, turning their personal development (even on a fundamental level that they see as positive) to align with the organization's larger vision.

Influence is a quiet power, observing underfoot while steering things before they arrive. Exerting influence requires extensive knowledge of situations, behind-the-scenes orchestration, and the appropriate conditions, including sequential flow, for the nudge to take effect—which doesn't happen in a vacuum.

In a knowledgeable organization, influence does not flow only top-down or up-bottom; it flows organically throughout the structure. After enough acceptance and support, influence becomes inscribed in the organizational DNA as a way of being to which team members may not even realize they are conforming.

How influence reaches beyond the moment is comparable to writing a persuasive text—likewise, organizational intelligence functions in a cycle of knowledge sharing, learning, and collective improvement. I have witnessed countless instances, both in formal and informal discussions, benefitting from input from different perspectives, even those off-collar whims. Every voice and experience enriches our collective understanding and fosters a vibrant debate. Accurate insights come—sharing in those moments, especially when they are considerably challenging. Experience is essential: as substantial and impressive as formal education may be, it's a good reminder never to discount the power of collective team knowledge. Degrees and certificates merely indicate a completed learning journey—natural intelligence in and of an organization comes from team members constantly learning, exchanging views, and weaving stories together.

Organizations by themselves are complex, dynamic ecosystems that are not easy to classify and usually present problems with no straightforward solutions. The perfect solution for one org will be far from a fit for others, and the road to an intelligent and collaborative business is never perfectly straight. The nonlinear path is also why use case discussion can be inappropriate; it's completely aligned with someone else's organization and isn't "how we do it." Therein lies the thrill of fostering alignment—not solely around goals and objectives but also in the shared values and beliefs underpinning what the organization stands for. Organizations flex and change, and the behavioral implications are often unaccounted for because it's forced rather than reimagined.

Recent events, such as the COVID crisis, have presented many challenges, such as budget cuts, and directly changed the typical on-site work landscape. Along with the shift to working remotely, there have been challenges in providing education assistance, access to conferences and training, and even team-building events. While the industry has started reimagining these events, it needs more adequate employee motivation. If you want an expert-level team, ensure they can feel like experts at your company and in the community.

Challenges aside, organizational intelligence transcends knowledge or skills, giving everyone a voice to be heard by others and an opportunity to learn and grow from others. It is an adventure in the purest sense to a location unknown but with rewards beyond measure. It's worth remembering the inevitable maturation of collaboration based on a shared experience predicated on progress. While we have heavily leaned into this in theory and practice collective intelligence (the community being smarter than individuals), organizational intelligence goes a step further, honing in on how organizations collect and process information to manage decisions. It has also, and will continue to, change how technology and people interact with intelligent systems. Innovative systems are expanding our capabilities by processing massive data sets, taking on repetitive tasks automatically, and aiding in globalization communication. As extensions of our collaborative minds, innovative systems enable new ways to work and expand what is possible.

Throughout history, organizations have witnessed distinct individual opinions hindering collective thought—even if it's simple derailment or intentional self-fulfillment. Thankfully, technology is helping to provide a medium to share and collaborate on these opinions-sharing pathways to make decision making more coherent. Yet, a change in thinking at that organizational level is required to leverage this digital age's opportunities, and organizational self-reflection marks the start of this journey. Leaders, teams, and individuals must evaluate their current levels of collective intelligence and areas for improvement. It is an invitation to move from notational knowledge, the sum of individual understandings about a problem or process, to collective mastery and collaboration with convergent technologies. Organizations that embrace this shift will discover their true potential. Collaborative intelligence at the organizational level accelerates decision making, deepens impact, and drives continuous evolution, which can create a more resilient, creative, and prosperous future.

It's not just a sweet spot where your organization can benefit from cross-functional learning; it also supports novelty in ideas and technologies. And that, right there, is the organizational maturity paradox. The following sections will explore principles and tactics for achieving the organization's balance of stability and agility, from fostering a culture of ongoing learning and flexibility to instigating new technologies while keeping your strength intact—ultimately, how to unleash intelligence across the organization.

Tackling the Organizational Maturity Paradox

Growth isn't just a choice anymore; it's a fundamental requirement for companies to prosper and for individuals to realize their full potential. The ability to transition from a small team to a global enterprise like Walmart, with millions of employees, is a clear testament to the power of growth. The intelligent investor admires and acquires shares in companies with expanding sales, improved margins, and streamlined processes. Regrettably, even as companies strive for growth, communication often remains fragmented, hampering the efficient flow of information vital for everyday operations and underscoring the urgent need for adequate and effective (for the organization) communication strategies.

Just as a chain's strength is determined by its weakest link, the success of the AI era hinges on the seamless integration of people, processes, and technology. In the interest of organizational strength, if leaders fail to provide education and contextual support to every team member, regardless of role, leaders inadvertently limit the potential of the entire organization. Of course, specialization is necessary and requires experts supervised by leaders who can integrate contributions into the bigger picture. As we look toward scaling the organization, do leaders prioritize the best candidate for a specific task or focus on those who align with the organization's values? It's likely a combination of both, but how do we ensure everyone progresses and grows together?

If you're part of a company, considering joining one, or even learning in a university setting, understanding an organization's level of data-driven decision making is crucial. Furthermore, you have to ensure that what you're looking at doesn't refer to the maturity of individual team members but rather how well the team members work together to leverage data and analytics for decision making.

Whether intended or not, Gartner's 2012 Analytics Maturity Model aimed to assess, or at least expose, the technology required to assess data-driven decision making. A mere six years later, in 2018,

A worldwide survey of 196 organizations by Gartner, Inc. showed that 91 percent of organizations have not yet reached a transformational level of maturity in data and analytics, despite this area being a number one investment priority for CIOs in recent years.[16]

Gartner acknowledged that this theoretical model didn't translate well into real-world practice. A glaring discrepancy highlights a key challenge: bridging the gap between theory and practice, between models and actual organizational behavior, demanding more than technical capabilities or individual expertise. It requires a supportive organizational fabric that fosters collaboration, knowledge sharing, and data-driven decision making at all levels. The road to analytical maturity is paved with challenges, but the rewards are significant. Organizations can unlock their full potential and thrive in an increasingly competitive landscape by cultivating a culture of data-driven insights and aligning individual efforts with organizational goals. Leaning on Gartner's model for understanding, here are some questions from each maturity level to evaluate where your organization stands:

Descriptive: Is the organization's focus primarily on describing past events across different aspects of the operation?

Diagnostic: Does the organization understand the why behind what happened?

Predictive: Can the organization forecast what's likely to occur with a high level of statistical certainty?

Prescriptive: Does the organization offer specific action recommendations based on one or more predictions?

Even analytically mature organizations lack situational awareness and context to support independent and unmonitored execution when using predictions. Having contextual data leads to certainty, and excess information may lead in the wrong direction due to overconfidence. *CIO* magazine has a great article about ten high-profile AI failures that illustrate an important point: AI has potential beyond the imagination, but because all these AI algorithms are based on data, from chatbots spewing less-than-true data, biased recruitment tools, and even AI-generated content posing as human work, the examples cited are a sobering reminder of why human oversight for contextual understanding is critical when crafting (and rolling out) AI systems.[17] Ideally, the organization can blend historical and institutional knowledge, predictive models, and situational awareness when approaching decisions.

Unfortunately, we're far away from that, and while most organizations have multiple analytic tools, they are stuck with basic reporting. Successful forecasting involves not only successfully predicting the future in a variety of scenarios but also being able to operationalize those insights into processes; effectively, all this forecasting activity is taken and used as an instrument within more mature operations—somewhat akin to having your very own working crystal ball at every interaction and every endpoint.

Reflect and Evaluate: Individual Versus Organizational Analytical Maturity

If you are curious to understand how mature your organization is from an analytical perspective, step back, way back, and watch.

> Often, the reason you can't see the solution because you're too close to the problem. Zoom out a little, zoom out a LOT and look at the big picture. This is a phenomenon similar to what psychologists call "cognitive restructuring"—shifting the way in which your problems are presenting themselves....[18]

Figure 3.1 The path to insights: A visual metaphor

Compare the activities you witness to your analytical thinking. If the way you think was described as an express elevator, it would be shooting up and down floors, analyzing problems along with the high speed of solving them, and sometimes seeming to skip steps due to prior knowledge. Individuals have mental shortcuts and models that allow anticipation and subsequent action (Figure 3.1).

Viewing the organization from afar, maturity looks more like a staircase—each step representing a level in the journey. The contrast can be stark. Organizations trail individual ways of thinking, meandering through those long-distributed reporting paths and organizational structures. When directly compared to individual capability, it exposes the need and desire to enable organizations to think and act as quickly and effectively as their most talented employees.

The Gartner Analytical Maturity Model has been very valuable in showcasing desired analytical capabilities alongside the tooling required to support each behavior. Unfortunately, as required levels of analytical sophistication leap forward, the model becomes increasingly too rudimentary.

Remember the subpart about individual versus organizational maturity that our previous discussion alluded to? Analytics is something individuals can navigate with ease. During a trip to the coffee shop, we see a crash and think, "What happened?" and immediately slow down, ensuring we don't end up in the same situation. Our minds, with impressive neural networks, are more potent than any organization because of its many people, processes, and technology. Our primary reaction, or immediate action, demonstrates a popular fallacy: even though everything is well and we are all working correctly, we immediately rush from descriptive facts to action without a more profound analysis. Even though we are incredibly interested, rubbernecking to see the details, in scenarios like this, we fail to look deeper into the "why." Other than avoiding it, it's unnecessary for our path forward.

Context is essential for each analysis stage, from descriptive analytics to predictive insights. As analytics become more sophisticated, context allows us to target more precisely so that data doesn't bury us. Context breeds confidence that our actions are moving us in the right direction by allowing us to be targeted in our decision making and ensuring we can easily align everything with our ultimate goals.

As technology improves, it generates deeper analytical insights from an ever-increasing swath of systems spanning multiple stages and workflows, aka various contexts. Remember the true essence of insights. A descriptive report's context changes when higher analytics levels are added. With that, it's critical to know the difference between descriptive data—a look back in time—and predictive insights—an informed view of potential futures. Awareness and differentiation are foundational to team members making the right decisions, dodging hurdles, and jumping on new possibilities.

Embracing Contextual Awareness in AI: A Path to Influence

Contextual awareness enhances predictive modeling. By incorporating context, we shift focus from solely analyzing past events to creating a statistically supported framework for anticipating future scenarios. Predictive models inform of future behaviors in support of our focus and surrounding context. A critical distinction arises when the future is known, and opportunity is unveiled. We're excited and ask, "When should we act on this knowledge?" Exposing the contrast between the moment we analyze the situation and the moment we have the power to change it. Recognizing these as crucial components in planning and execution, we can define them as the Point of Analysis and the Point of Influence. For further understanding, here's a question highlighting each:

> The point of analysis is when we actively examine available information to understand the current situation and anticipate potential developments. It's about gathering insights and knowledge to inform our decision-making process.
> The point of influence is a strategic juncture where we can actively support a motionless means of interaction to shape events. It is where we can implement guidelines, leverage situational

and environmental resources, and support decisions that will proactively guide desired outcomes.

Organizational influence architecture artistry finds critical leverage points where nurturing guidance supports positive outcomes for the organization and the audience in some way, shape, or form. Influential support is not an intervention; it is best provided as a subtle and motionless addition. We can formulate behaviorally relevant models in specific contexts by understanding and identifying these influence points within workflows or organizational interactions. Contextually relevant models combined with contextually aware AI can detect all the nuances and cover adequate reactions in different scenarios. An AI system's usefulness varies widely depending on its position in the operational workflow. It should be well-poised to read the most pertinent incoming information and take actions that propagate desired ripple effects.

Contextual awareness is not just about training our AI models but also about deploying them saliently. In other words, every AI instance should react according to environmental change. By doing so, adequately deployed AI remains on track and fulfills its purpose inside a previously unforeseen sphere.

The last and seemingly lost, or unconsciously assumed, ingredient required is the development of system-wide information and actionability. A proper ecosystem permits AI to kick off cascading effects across down-the-line events and processes in synchronization with up-the-line influence points. While constantly aware but seemingly dormant, your contextually aware AI system collects data and listens to sensors, shuffling through logic over silicon to wake up from inactive sleep and support a simple and timely nudge. There is so much anticipation; finally, AI delivers precisely as intended.

In the context of one model, such orchestrated alignment across the organization demands sophisticated systems that can accumulate, manage, and understand myriad contextual information. Allowing the AI to learn, predict, and redesign its behavior based on expected outcomes helps it become more valuable and impactful.

Data processing should not be the future of AI; rather, it should be able to comprehend the context behind that data. AI will then transition into something more than just an observer; it will be a catalyst shaping the future with confident and context-specific action.

Take a moment to make this real; consider the simple task of brewing coffee. Contextually aware AI could elevate a mundane experience to a personalized and delightful one. Imagine saying, "Alexa, make me a cup of coffee." A straightforward instruction would trigger intelligent actions to brew coffee and craft your perfect cup. Dig deeper into this reality:

AI's contextual comprehension—understanding preferences: The AI, having learned your preferences over time, would know your ideal coffee strength, roast, milk, sugar choices, and even the optimal brewing temperature.

AI's multicontext adaptation: To personalize the brewing process further, contextual factors such as the time of day, your current activity level, or even the weather could be considered. For instance, it might suggest a more potent brew in the morning to boost your energy or a decaf option in the evening to promote restful sleep.

AI's extensive insights—anticipating needs: A contextually aware AI that supports making your coffee could even anticipate your needs before you express them. For instance, it might notice your low coffee supply and proactively order more beans or pods.

It's a simple example of contextual awareness's power in AI, enabling machines to move beyond simple task execution and deliver truly personalized and meaningful experiences that enhance our lives in countless ways.

The Power of Contextual AI

AI is getting better and better at doing specific tasks, like predicting yes or no or generating a response. However, AI still needs to be more flexible and able to handle different situations, as humans can understand the context of a problem and respond appropriately. This means contextual AI can handle more complex tasks and adapt to

Figure 3.2 Evolution of humans and technology: A visual narrative

new challenges. Contextual AI can revolutionize how we interact with technology. Imagine having a conversation with your AI assistant that's as natural and intuitive as talking to a friend or using your AI assistant to help you with complex tasks, like planning a trip or managing your finances. The potential of contextual AI is enormous, as it can make our lives easier, more productive, and more enjoyable (Figure 3.2).

Organizations investing in AI systems prioritizing context will likely be better positioned to achieve harmony. Beyond the AI era is a period that involves leveraging combined forces of humans and machines. For organizations, this means unveiling tomorrow's machineforce while balancing it with the workforce to maximize collective potential. Communicating our needs, preferences, and goals to AI allows us to personalize interactions, automate tasks, and unlock insights. The partnership extends beyond personalization, optimizing AI to enhance our actions and unleash untapped potential. Imagine a world where learning is accelerated, decisions are more intelligent, and innovation flourishes. Those who embrace the synergy will gain a significant advantage in the increasingly clever and competitive market. By developing AI technologies that understand us, we can harness technology for the betterment of humanity. A supportive machineforce isn't a choice; it's our inevitable future.

Bridging the Data and Decision Gap

With technology and data inextricably linked—but also frequently compartmentalized across many different silos—we live in a world where the pace of business moves faster than almost ever before. And while technology has made progress in opening some of these silos, real innovation requires more than just aggregating data into a central store. Most organizations that embrace new technology do so quickly without revisiting the core business processes. Like the natural world, data and information within organizations will always be present in multiple states, integrated or siloed (especially if security is a concern). Organizations face the challenge of using innovative technologies to drive performance while maintaining security and control.

Advanced analytic solutions bring the power to collect data from different sources, including but not limited to providing continuous business insight. In all amazement, it is easy to lose sight of the most under-estimated art—information governance, not data science or algorithms. Organizing, cataloging, and distributing data appropriately is a nightmare that is becoming further complicated by international regulations.

Sometimes, the organization's most valuable information is like a secret agent on a mission—it needs to be mobile and ready for anything. The organization's little AI robots are versions of Ethan Hunt, except instead of impossible missions, they're tackling complex tasks with a need for crucial background info embedded in them, like a built-in cheat sheet so that they can adapt to different situations. Unlike those messages in Mission Impossible movies, this data won't self-destruct— it's there to stay and help them succeed.

Bridging the governance gap is more complex than data distribution and integration, so a laid-out strategy must be implemented and continuously managed. On a positive note, it presents an opportunity to comprehend the intricate web of information that flows through the organization. Understanding who all these pivotal decision makers are and ensuring they have access to accurate, contextually relevant data in a timely fashion require extensive knowledge of business requirements, technology capabilities, and integration possibilities to systematically distribute information that supports proactive organizational enrichment.

Navigating the Thin and Wide

Recognizing the gap between business and IT seems logical, but doing something about the situation requires more than accepting it. With the rise of the consumerized facade, IT carves up data as information is demanded from various audiences, seeking only a small piece of what could be made available. In cases where the organization has no internal expertise, it may also look to outsource the work required. Outsourcing is not without issue—when consultants walk out the door, so does their valuable expertise: not in what they brought to your organization but in what they helped develop at your organization. It's crucial to recognize that you don't want to rely on temporary resources to form the talent that can help grow your company long term. Recognition of supporting workforce assets should align with two specific roles: workforce extensions and knowledge accelerators.

Workforce extensions support the organization in the spirit of staff augmentation by engaging consultants for specific, clearly defined projects where their unique expertise can offer quick wins. The organization ensures that the extended resources participate and that a permanent employee shadows and owns the work, retaining the organization's information.

Positioned as coaches and educators, **knowledge accelerators** ensure that essential business knowledge is passed on to internal team members, establishing a sustainable foundation for future success.

To safeguard interests, ensure that skills and expertise are transferred or that new, homegrown capabilities are ready to take over when outsourcing occurs. Knowledge management should be integral to your business structure and closely aligned with IT.

Embracing a New Era of Interaction

Engagement today differs from before technology, especially artificial intelligence (AI), took over. Every interaction is seemingly unseen until it blows up in front of us. Today's interactions can be completely different tomorrow or even minutes later. Although not aligned just yet, consistency matters. As AI systems move from automation tools to fundamental components of business operations, supporting contextual frameworks and internal knowledge repositories will help ensure consistency and reliability in every interaction and preserve historical information. Ultimately, whether this is done by a central AI monitoring organizational interaction or through individual AI solutions being closely aligned, it should be the same: provide one organizationally supported experience at the point of interaction by human and machine alike.

An interactive need furthers the requirement for AI systems to have contextual and situational awareness, especially when tracing points of influence to outcomes. In the same way that a reasonable employee would adjust behavior when faced with unique challenges, AI systems must provide nuanced responses and go deeper into reasoning by showing that expectations are genuinely acknowledged. Even a polite variant, such as "I cannot respond to that," is somewhat disheartening and may deter future participation.

Transitioning to an AI-powered organization requires a drastic change in how organizations model interactions. It requires somewhat of a red-thread strategy that guides the efforts of humans and machines while maintaining consistency in responsiveness in every available channel—made straight by one voice. An approach that will reassure the audience that they are on the right path to leveraging the power of AI. It all begs the question; how do you manage that alignment between humans and machines in your enterprise?

Digital Libraries: The Cornerstone of Knowledge-Driven Organizations

Beyond interactions, we're also drowning in data. The flood of information has transformed the way organizations function, and data are no longer just an asset; it truly becomes what keeps companies alive and drives them forward. Raw data are a small bounty in the same manner that crude oil is useless if not refined. Being able to extract, process, and —most importantly—understand data in the proper context becomes mighty! It might surprise you that the opportunity isn't necessarily intelligent machines but the appropriate information curation to support a knowledgeable path forward.

In this light, context reigns supreme and is precisely where the importance of having an internal digital library comes into play. Beyond a simple electronic repository, a well-crafted digital library becomes an actively alive knowledge temple that reflects the nuanced functional-ities—within business systems—that are valuable to execute strategic action. It captures the data and all that valuable context—who created it, when, why, and how it was built in the first place or over time. Holistic, in that it unifies the human employees with their AI systems to work synergistically and drive every single decision derived from a clear and complete understanding of available info and securely steer the organization forward on its strategic objectives.

Your digital library is the beating heart of your organizational knowledge base. It is a central repository in which information is stored and immediately curated to enable each team and individual in the organization. While a public library may grant generally open access, a digital library provides more of an enriched experience aimed at providing information relevant to that user's specific needs and responsibilities. Information is stored and displayed to multiple perspectives around the organization, ensuring the proper knowledge is available, promoting efficiency and informed decision making. In addition, the digital library should include data sets and a vast major-ity (if possible) of resources such as reference materials and standard operating procedures, among other templates crucial for completing day-to-day work. For instance, if a customer service representative is working on an individual inquiry, they should be able to review the associated procedure and all necessary forms or templates. Removing the risk of having to weave back and forth across systems should cut down on both errors in interpretation and misfiling.

Empowering Users With AI-Enhanced Workflows

Consistent usage patterns help organizations to integrate AI into their workflows seamlessly. Suppose an AI module replaces a manual process.

Rather than interfering with the flow of events for a user, the digital library changes just in time. The routine process page opens for the user. Instead of getting a manual form to fill out—they get an AI-enhanced solution that simplifies the chore—and either walks them through specific required measurements or does some level of automation—a synergistic experience where the machineforce melds in with the workforce. In support of a frictionless experience, mind these key takeaways:

Curation is key: Curate the digital library's content meticulously to ensure each user receives information tailored precisely to their role and needs, empowering them with the most relevant and actionable insights.

Go beyond data: Organize various assets like procedures, templates, and reference materials in a structured and progressive manner. Break down information into levels—primary, advanced, and expert—to facilitate understanding and cater to different skill sets within the organization. A conversational approach ensures comprehensive support for all aspects of work.

Embrace AI integration: Leverage AI to automate tasks and provide guidelines supporting interactive and streamlined workflows, seamlessly integrating it into the digital library experience.

Empower users: Provide employees with the proper tools, information, and, most importantly, guidelines to make informed decisions and contribute to the organization's success.

By building a digital library that fosters knowledge sharing, collaboration, and AI integration, organizations can create a more empowered, efficient, and adaptable workforce ready to tackle the challenges of the digital age. A well-structured digital library should include:

Intuitive structure: A clear and organizationally relevant categorization system, like the Dewey Decimal System, ensures easy navigation and information retrieval.

Powerful asset catalog: A robust, searchable index enabling users to locate specific information quickly. The asset catalog is an opportunity to give every individual their view of the information at hand.

Flexible storage options: These options accommodate handling large or uniquely formatted data and prevent limitations due to file size or type. It's essential to understand that this is not an architectural recommendation; store the data however you wish and ensure the proper experience for the end users.

Rich contextual details: Besides basic metadata, this includes summaries, usage notes, and peer reviews to enhance understanding and facilitate informed use of assets.

Organizational alignment and tagging: A crucial feature for large organizations is identifying the relevant department, project, or initiative associated with each asset, promoting collaboration and knowledge sharing.

All the features listed above combine to create a digital library that is not merely a repository of information but a dynamic tool that supports knowledge discovery, collaboration, and decision making within the organization. One that evolves alongside your organization. Changes in how data are generated, used, and named should be reflected in the system over time. Remember, metadata is the DNA of your digital library, giving depth, relevance, context, and completion to each data asset and includes details such as:

Descriptors and tags: Definitions of the data, structure, and constraints, including organizationally relevant context, collection activities, contextual relevance, and so on. These should be expressed as actual descriptions and categorized with tags.

Access control: Granular permissions to secure and comply with data with operational access, specifying who can access what.

Usage and systems integration: Usage and systems integration provides an organization with transparency, traceability, and understanding of data usage. Organizations can improve data

management practices, reduce risk, and ensure compliance by
mapping data flows between systems, itemizing usage, and
establishing traceability.

Usage patterns: Information on how the data is accessed, by whom,
and for what specific value or trend points in a clear direction
around where potential optimization can occur.

Data lineage: A complete map of the data, where it came from, and
its transformations to ensure traceability and promote trust while
supporting sound decision making using Data provenance.

Regulatory compliance: Regulatory compliance ensures that an
organization's data management practices comply with all
applicable laws and regulations, protecting the organization from
legal penalties, reputational damage, and loss of trust.

Unlocking the Potential of Data

Your internal digital library is much more than a backup in the age
of AI. It is a strategic asset that seeds innovation, powers efficiency,
and ultimately results in durable success. Ultimately, businesses need to
ensure they can access and understand their data so that it becomes a
competitive advantage—but sweeping your information under the rug
will never give you an edge in this brave new world. Creating a deep,
contextual digital library will open the door to your data's full potential
and result in:

Improved decision making: Teams with quick access to trustworthy
and contextually relevant data can make fast, confident decisions—static parties.

Collaboration: A unified library of reusable data elements allows the
organization to share information and collaborate across internal
departments, reducing fragmented (or siloed) pools that tend to
grow around random-access connections.

Increased efficiency: More streamlined access to their data leaves
organizations with more time for other work, increasing
productivity.

Enhanced security: Granular access controls and detailed metadata secure sensitive data, helping businesses comply with regulatory requirements.

Cultivating a Transformative Mindset

The widespread distribution of free AI has left executive leaders anxious. Discomfort arises from a concern about losing power to AI, making decision makers out of everyone, and favoring short-term benefits due to focused predictions versus broader organizational health.

Using AI-driven decision making also conflicts spectacularly with regulatory compliance. An organization must ensure the AI systems they implement have a legal side to them. Ultimately, however, any decision made with the help of AI needs to be transparent and explainable—requiring a more detailed understanding of how these models work their mechanisms internally (because in extensive complexity, they are mainly black boxes to us common folk), what data were used for training them, and if they can have biases toward some potential aspects.

The complicated reality is that analytical maturity is more than a complex linear continuum. It is a fluid, always-changing thing. Prescriptive insights, or "what to do" recommendations, depend highly on the foundational information created at lower maturity levels (descriptive and diagnostic analysis). They form intricate relationships without essential stages, and advancement lies in an iterative feedback loop. When parts of a firm lead and other areas lag, operations will be fragmented with inconsistent interactions.

Decisive leadership is required to determine what the organization should do about its current efforts and a detailed vision of where AI could lead if plotted on an organizational roadmap. In the AI Era, authentic leadership requires more than just long-term strategizing—it demands planting a transformational vision in your team, and this doesn't equate to a wholesale change but creating the right environment for sharing, teaming, and learning. To help navigate changes, leaders must lead their teams (imagine that), share victories, and encourage everyone involved along this journey.

Addressing the Gap and Cultivating an Insight-Driven Culture

To start with, adopting AI is problematic because people don't know what it offers. While everyone is excited about the possibilities, it's yet to be framed in such a way that supports business usage. The idea that machine learning builds models is fantastic. Still, most business team members are unaware that the model is a response to a question, like yes or no (technically termed binary classification). Leaders must encourage open dialogue and provide educational support to build on AI's role in the organization. Every time you hear the phrase "The AI will do that," it should trigger additional questions for leaders to address:

> Which AI, specifically? Informing decisions requires an understanding of the AI system used.
>
> What exactly will it do? Leaders must specify the tasks and functions AI should accomplish so everyone realizes its position within the procedure.
>
> How will our process operate as people interact with it? Define steps where AI fits into the existing human workflow and which responsibilities are covered, stressing the partnership between both.
>
> What about when the AI is not working? Create robust contingency plans and fail-safes if an AI system fails or becomes obsolete so businesses can continue with minimal disruption.

"Humans can no longer afford to think in division and darkness. Collaborative Intelligence is the light that is necessary for our individual and collective survival. We have no choice but to think together."[19] That is, having conversations every time AI comes up to augment or replace current processes. By doing so, leaders can communicate that AI is more than a deep-rooted misinterpretation of automating work, something that's crucial to developing this changing mindset. By providing a simple and direct focus, AI can drive a culture where data-driven insights are valued, giving stakeholders comfort that AI is not meant to replace humans but to augment capabilities and improve efficiency.

Behavioral Benchmarks: Evaluating Processes and Maturity

To drive significant change, know the organization: what makes it tick, what it does and does not do, and how decisions are made. Most of the emphasis seems to focus on how to mature analytically, but it is critical that organizations also examine the organizational processes that support maturity. Developed initially at Carnegie Mellon, the Capability Maturity Model Integration (CMMI) is a helpful model for evaluating organizational behavior.[20]

CMMI provides a framework for appraising your organization's processes and helps you improve them. Central to this construct is organizing key processes into five maturity levels, each representing increased capability. While the roots of CMMI are in terms related to project management, explicitly tracking project achievements concerning timeliness and quality while tackling cost concerns, it can be morphed into a bird of all feathers by assessing an organization's analytical maturity in any value stream that calls for several technical disciplines. CMMI provides a means for evaluating an organization's behavior and practices (as well as, with appropriate analytic maturity, what an organization may be able to do in the future) through a

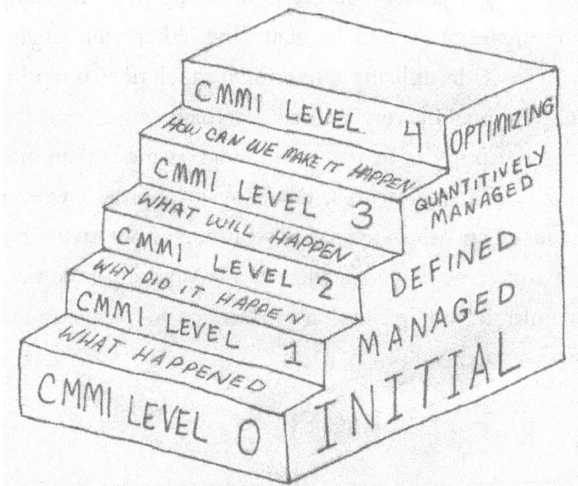

Figure 3.3 Critical steps: Capability and behavior

consistent frame. CMMI does this by assessing tools and processes—asking critical questions about how the organization functions and what it can do in the future (Figure 3.3).

The Gartner Analytical Maturity Model described in the book offers a complementary view of the capabilities needed to progress along the CMMI-determined maturity levels. Integrating CMMI with the Analytical Maturity Model allows organizations to evaluate their analytical capabilities against behavioral characteristics and the fact that these capabilities reinforce good behavior. It's a cautious reminder that the technologies you use, build, and deploy will dictate how your organization grows and behaves. Consider your organization the most complicated machine, which allows you to think of your tools as gears and levers. That said, having the tools in place doesn't magically produce results; evidence suggests it's about how those tools work together within the system that counts.

CMMI serves as a road map to determine the maturity of your organizational processes, and the Analytical Maturity Model helps you understand how well you can use data for better decisions and actions. Together, they serve as a powerful "sanity check"—enabling you to determine how your investments in technology and analytical talent transform desired behavior patterns and outcomes. As the organization moves on the combined staircase, think with fresh perspectives by imagining looking at a target rather than seeing it as the straight path between the organization and its goal. The closer your organizational behavior aligns with utilizing prescriptive analytics to optimize, the more accurately you'll hit your bullseye (strategic objectives).

Fulfilling the promise of new technology is more than automating what we now do; it represents a new way to approach work and life. When you focus on behavior change, why not shoot at the bullseye of analytical maturity while you're there, too? Anything becomes possible when you unleash your technology in service to purposeful organizational growth.

Extending the Digital Library: A Repository for Contextual Decisions

Information flow across and external to the organization is challenging to handle, and data should be universally intelligible, but this would only gel slowly with requirements for standardization or individualization. Generally, the newer members of teams will look for something in data structures or might even think of making one if they find an existing piece. Filtering out this well-meaning noise is to stop legitimate information from flowing and collaborating. A more nuanced approach is required, one that objectively examines the reasons for changing content. Are their interpretations of the data correct compared to those of the original (Figure 3.4)?

One way to handle complexity is by expanding the notion of a digital library and introducing a contextual decision repository. As an expanded feature, it's like a sports replay system that gives you all the angles and viewpoints to grasp how these decisions are made. The expansion promotes a culture of transparency, accountability, and ongoing learning for the organization. It is an asset that the entire

Figure 3.4 The library of decisions: A glimpse into the augmented world

organization can leverage by learning from past efforts and making better future decisions. Included in the decision repository are things like:

Decision history: A log of past decisions, including who made them, when, and why.

Information context: The specific data points or insights informed each decision.

Outcome analysis: Reporting and summaries that examine the impact and results of each decision, providing valuable feedback for future decision making.

Alternative scenarios: Document alternative paths considered but not taken and the rationale for those choices.

Navigating the Data Deluge: Unveiling Clarity

It's overwhelming between the dashboards and charts and information everywhere in our data-soaked world. When it comes to data, we often get too caught up in what a piece of information is on the surface and miss how compelling insights are derived from manipulating the raw form. It's about probing, asking more questions, and what is the claim from which the source of information commenced, all activities where insight literacy becomes critical.

Stepping back, data literacy is knowing what different types of data (retrospective or static, predictive, or prescriptive) are and how they are created. Insight literacy takes it a step further, giving the ability to make judgments and see evidence for their worth—one second-class data representation or another? Most importantly, it allows us to understand from different vantage points in which data have been illustrated to see the extended picture.

The notion of "curated data" could not be more critical in support of the organization and, with it, the understanding that few of us talk, write, and discuss data in a neutral, objective way. It's gathered and typically compiled or cherrypicked (depending on how you look at it) to push specific arguments/narratives. Knowledge of the methods to curate the data is essential to insight literacy. Understanding the maturity levels and perspectives inherent in data visualizations allows us to communicate our insights clearly and confidently, resulting in more effective teamwork and decision making.

Insight literacy is not asking for a heads-down revolution; it can grow naturally within your analytics ecosystem. Every time you update a dashboard or visualization, treat it like an opportunity to onboard its corresponding insight compass. A simple visual becomes a lighthouse of transparency, telling everyone the data are cleaned, curated, prepared, and can be trusted. An insight compass and organizational understanding ensure the correct interpretation of information. Here are some keys in support of expanding data and insight literacy beyond academic understanding:

Visual storytelling: The language of intuition: Subtle design choices wield surprising power. For instance, color palettes can highlight essential data points, well-chosen icons can add context to the visualization, and clear labels can provide additional information. When woven into your visualizations, these elements tell a story immediately. Faded colors might whisper about less precise data, while a bold question mark sparks curiosity and further investigation. We've all learned to associate visuals with emotions and actions—use this to your advantage! By carefully crafting your visualizations, you can influence your workforce to grasp the data and align their behaviors accordingly intuitively.

Context is king: The power of metadata: Descriptive labels and visualization keys are your allies! Detail the data's origin, potential limitations, and how it was gathered. Transparency fosters trust and gives users the context they need for sound decision making. Remember, data are subjective and open to different perspectives; contextual metadata helps everyone get on the same page. The imagery of the capture points, along with the interfaces, can also be powerful contextual support.

Knowledge is power: Fostering a learning culture: Training initiatives are essential for a data-savvy organization. Focus on data and insight literacy. Equip everyone, from analysts to executives, with the critical thinking tools they need. Encourage questions like "What are the assumptions behind this?" or "Could this data have other meanings?"

With these supportive strategies in place, empower a shift within your organization. Data stop being merely visualized and start being deeply understood. The insight compass and these guiding principles become the road signs of the information landscape. Your workforce confidently navigates complexity, makes informed choices, and feels less burdened by the uncertainty that raw data can present. This ultimately frees them up to think strategically and unleash their problem-solving potential.

Insight Shortcuts: The Power of an Insight Compass

Data visualizations are potent means of uncovering hidden patterns and triggering momentous decisions. However, the ever-increasing complexity is a double-edged sword, as it creates ambiguity and can leave room for misinterpretation. A single attractive but misleading visualization, taken outside the proper context and adequately interpreted, can wreak havoc.

Your organization's "insight compass"—a simple directional addition for each dashboard helps tremendously. A visualization that indicates the maturity level of findings from the curator. In other words, end users could immediately comprehend if insights are descriptive, diagnostic, predictive, or prescriptive. Developing basic terminology beyond technical jargon allows the content of your data to become digestible by more users with trivial knowledge about its potential. Whether it is the simplest of labels, a status bar, or some more sophisticated diagram … it is there to be remembered. How good (or not) the insights are steer clarity toward informed choices. There is no one-size-fits-all for your compass design, but it is worth considering these keys:

Simplicity: Ensure that everyone understands everything briefly by the end of each insight section or visualization. Avoid intricate visualizations that take a long time to explain.

Visibility: The compass should be prominent but manageable relative to the primary data.

Adaptability: Create an adaptable compass, that is, different maturity levels and data types.

Integration: Ensure your insight compass fits your current visual formatting and supports the mental shortcuts desired for each view (Figure 3.5).

An insight compass can revolutionize your organization's use of data by improving and accelerating decision making. Users can quickly assess whether data are fit for purpose. It can support increased understanding and lessen the danger of immature conclusions being misrepresented. As a stamp of approval and maturity, it provides transparency around data maturity and increases trust in existing processes. It can also provide more precise communication as it builds a shared perspective for all and a joint understanding of the insights displayed.

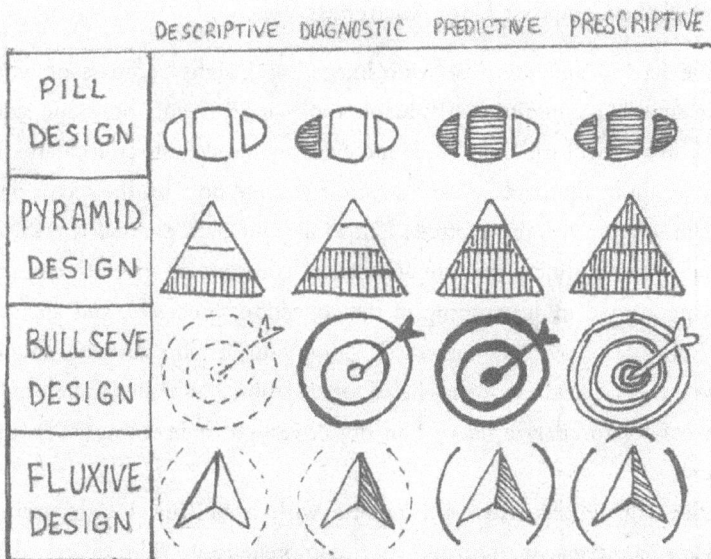

Figure 3.5 Insight compass examples

Implementing an insight compass can also be organizationally charged—something great for the organization. You can choose to name your directional asset—and discuss the implications with leadership on how you can position what is simply a way of talking about doing qualitative future work for directive alignment. Your insight compass, on-target key, or perhaps a supportive evidence gauge.... It ought to be something that reflects your style of organization. This is another thing to be very careful about, as you specify precisely what each maturity level in the model means within your context. If you even question how to use it, pilot with a team and get feedback. Sequence yourselves. A test with the compass on a small user group will ensure your updates based on their feedback, and you may get buy-in naturally by having champions in place to train the rest of the organization.

For example, a compass design with a scaled gauge or a simple color-coded bar like a horizontal bar divided into colored sections representing each of these levels. Or even a bull's eye with circles inside each other, the most mature data at our core. It would give the perception of maturity and intuition, too—in that closer means to ring; you are nearby, starting up.

Beyond the Compass: Data Awareness

While having an enterprise-wide image, an insight compass of what your data lake contains is a valuable tool—it represents only one side. Data literacy will still be critical, and everyone needs self-service data. Be curious about the data available; even if you are not "on the tech side," remember that context matters. Knowing your data context is critical, as we have outlined it with an insight compass to give us literacy. Having a good understanding of the collection, processes, and analysis is invaluable in any data analysis. Position your insights correctly so you have the exact alignment that helps for situational analysis. Therefore, it is necessary to analyze data in an objective light concerning goals and actions.

See your dashboards and reports with a built-in insight point-of-view compass. It informs your comprehension, illuminates data maturity, and shows where you could go further. When the understanding of what good looks like is shared, decisions are well-informed, confidence in your data grows, and you truly become a data-driven organization.

Embedding Influence in Daily Work

Domino's is one such company that has implemented creative ways to ensure the daily reality of life permeates all levels. As part of their test kitchen initiative, all employees, including the marketing and executive-level folks, must jump into the actual Domino's kitchen.[21] It's not just watching—they take orders, make pizzas, and test new methods. Doing this complete immersion has a massive upside.

Practicing genuine empathy as an executive and organizational leader can be challenging, but nothing beats knowing every person's job in your company—from R&D to accounts payable. Project work allows team members to see where the weak links are, what processes take longer than they should, and if some technologies aren't helping automate several workflows.

The test kitchen work perfectly illustrates how decisions made in the headquarters can directly translate into daily work. Innovation comes through fresh perspectives, including diverse backgrounds and divergent views. In the end, frontline experience can enable innovative efficiency improvements and further bridge the organization's end-to-end flow.

Although Domino's is a shining example, they are hardly the only ones taking this approach, and in truth, these principles extend beyond just food. A few other means of making it better:

Job shadowing: To bridge the gap by swapping places with admin and front-line people. This immersion experience has enabled administrative staff to see and feel the successes and challenges experienced by customer service frontline employees, which, in turn, fuels understanding. As the primary benefit, job shadowing builds empathy. The administrative staff understands better and values the day-to-day life of the front line, which makes their decision making also constructive in a larger sense. Shadowing can help improve communication by reducing silos and fostering inter-departmental dialogue. It can also boost morale when front-line employees know their work is recognized by those higher up in the food chain and truly valued.

Customer service rotations: Customer service interactions expose employees from different areas to customers directly via call centers (or other service channels). They can witness firsthand customer pain points, identify opportunities for continuous improvement, and develop insights into the customer's journey. This provides added customer understanding: Employees experience what customers are interested in, their issues, and requirements from the horse's mouth. It can also help problem-solving skills: Employees learn to comprehend and solve problems through direct customer interactions. Furthermore, these interactions can influence the development of products/services. Customer feedback during the rotations can be invaluable in developing or improving existing products and services, thereby increasing customer satisfaction.

Field visits: It motivates senior leadership and management to visit several different company locations, be they branches, stores, or factories, where the operations are done on a real-time basis and communicate with employees and customers at ground level. Insight into ground realities: Leaders get a first-hand perspective of how policies and strategies operate on the field. Increased employee engagement: Seeing leadership interested in and visiting their work shows they value what matters to them. These direct interactions create stronger bonds and relationships between leaders at all levels of the organization and their employees.

In a time of data saturation, unlock insights by breaking down silos, growing empathy, and refining the skills for learning. Searching for perspectives outside the mainstream leads to finding and addressing real problems and makes for better decision making overall.

CHAPTER 4

Harnessing AI's Invisible Power

Like master calligraphers use invisible brush strokes, artificial intelligence (AI) has and will continue to integrate effortlessly into the tapestry of our daily lives. AI is mighty yet has dual properties. It can change the scientific landscape and society when used ethically and responsibly. However, it can also be possible to abuse this influence without sufficient regulation or even unintentional excess. As such, we must approach AI's influence with the same reverence a Jedi has for the Force—a potent energy that, if left unchecked, can reshape the very foundations of our society.

Given that AI can and will influence behavior—bordering subconsciously at times, it may be time to check our ethical practices. Influence must be a "still touch" (gentle, user-in-control transparency). People deserve to know about the impact of their experiences and exercise choice (such as opting out). Finding the balance between individuality in personalization versus end user choice is critical to success. AI should make our lives better, not control them, and as such, some vital considerations are required:

Transparency: Openly communicating, even if just an indicator, when AI has supported, enhanced, or shaped our experience or behavior.

User control: Allowing users to configure their AI interactions and say no whenever they do not want recommendations.

Ethical frameworks: Create a robust set of organizational moral guidelines, even as a new way to attract your audience, for developing and deploying AI focusing on user health and well-being and outlaws manipulative practices.

Human oversight: Ensuring that an element of human involvement/prerequisite is featured in the decision-making process to ensure consistency with ethical standards and human values, and so on.

Relying on the principles outlined above, we can utilize AI positively without losing our freedom, making it essential for everyone to use and not corrupt individuals or institutions suitably. Whether it's a personal anecdote or a company-wide AI implementation, our daily experiences offer a lens into the true impact of AI, highlighting the crucial need for AI systems that are not only intelligent but also contextually aware and adaptive. AI stands to disrupt various industries and enhance our lives if it is carefully handled by adhering to ethical guidelines that guarantee its overall well-being while shielding us from out-of-control repercussions.

The fate of increasingly powerful technology is in our hands; its application depends on the code we write. Transparency, user control, ethical frameworks, and human oversight can lead to AI helping us work better together and empowering businesses that drive positive outcomes. As we move deeper into the AI age, let us watch carefully on all that may be gained and lost if this revolution is not guided wisely; a new frontier is passionate with potential but also fraught with perils of its own making.

Beneath the Surface: Decoding Undercurrents

Though we like to think of our actions as originating from free will, the truth is that the world turns to influence. A little push here, persuasion there, and soon … we imagine something or do something. It's easy to identify the blatant influences, like clever jingles, convincing commercials, and encouraging road signs that play a constant role in our daily lives. But what about more subtle, less evident forces?

The premise of influence architecture is that our beliefs are shaped by experiences cloaked in thoughts and their interactions. Even if the ambient temperature is excellent and certainly not cold enough to be concerned with changing back into clothes quickly, going from a hot tub to an unheated pool can easily inspire shock. Humans' contextualized thinking aligned with physical feelings demonstrates how we always make reference points and interpret the world one way or another.

Our ever-evolving thought processes are already complex but become even more intricate when we need to interact with others, and the experiences that color our responses are exclusive to each of us. One person's fascination is another one disinterest. When we want to sway someone, we naturally adjust and try to identify with how they think so we can find ways of communicating together. It's a dance of adaptation that shows how incredibly complex human relationships are. Our lives are delicate fabrics of subtle cues and triggers that shape our actions or inaction. We are influenced in countless ways, from barely perceptible cues in the environment to implicit social dynamics all around us.

Viewing influence from an organizational perspective holds fantastic promise. Using AI, the organization can create experiences that contextualize and bring moments together. It's not hard to imagine AI systems that recognize all your preferences and send the perfect text to recipients; we're pretty much doing that now. Even more remarkable is the ability to foster organizational growth by crafting an environment where subtle nudges guide behavior toward a desired outcome.

The first step is understanding that influence isn't about manipulation but recognizing the interplay between human perception and motivation. The more we tap into the subtle forces that shape human interaction, the more effective our communication becomes, opening up new possibilities for connection and collaboration. It's worth reviewing some of the many undercurrents in human behavior, beginning with learned behaviors:

> Learned behaviors: We learn to associate certain symbols with their meanings early on. Though their size may be shrinking, the octagonal design of a stop sign prompts an immediate response —we pause momentarily to check our surroundings before continuing. Traffic lights control how cars move, and red is known everywhere as a stop. Likewise, a flashing red light on the dashboard indicates things that could be wrong, so we investigate

them. These patterns create a language of interactions woven into the fabric of our day to day. AI routines might adapt to what we have built but can be used to dispel confusion.

Aligned, assimilated, and subconscious cues: Messages or cues are not always overt; sometimes, they operate below the radar of our conscious awareness yet still influence our actions. Think of a softly lit store with some chill music playing—an environment that inspires you to take three deep breaths. Without telling you that, this atmosphere does suggest a casual browsing experience. AI can heighten these subtleties, constructing tailored and immersive experiences. For example, an AI-driven e-commerce site might tailor the page colors and background music to what a customer has browsed. Lo-fi would help fuel sales of anything cozy, while joltier energy would sell activewear. Chatbots driven by AI can even mimic a user's most popular way of communicating, meaning they feel connected to the service and have the proper interactions that result in happier customers. AI could evolve to understand and replicate subtle human cues, helping those with challenges navigate their world more seamlessly. Taking this concept to another level, we all have a subconscious association (say, e.g., Bentley with wealth), but an artificial system with that info about millions of people would be interesting.

Physical behaviors and feelings: Predicting is a considerable advantage; understanding patterns and cues helps us do just that. To an extent, we can discern the white noise influencing our decision making. Our emotional perception of colors, shapes, and sounds. Red can mean excitement, urgency, or danger (which is why you see it in warning signs and sales offers). In contrast, spa ads usually use calming blues and greens to convey a calm sense.

Beyond the obvious: Language is a powerful force—the right word, inflection, or belief can alter what we see and how. Oh, it's so insidious! Think of a fiery orator turning to rhetoric and pathos (look it up if you will!) to manipulate the audience. Words have implications and meanings beyond the facts.

It's worth asking: Are we unintentionally making ourselves break by mood modification because our environment bullies our emotions? Are the bright colors and upbeat music (like a packed theme park) getting us pumped—priming us to make that purchase? Retail stores, naturally—store-littered endcaps and shoppable aisles fraught with temptation. Well, at this point, those online ads specific to you still following your every move will be slightly more unsettling. Today, the power of the digital world to impact the environment is pretty much a given.

Orchestrating the Artificial Hand of Influence

What if these tactics were pumped up on steroids and kept hidden in the shadows? Intelligent gadgets that watchfully analyze you and are out of control all the time, pulling you too focused here over there on products or ideas—nearly the whole thing is devoid of your awareness. Inevitably, we'd end up in the land of "dark patterns"—room for tech and psychology to conspire just subtly enough that only some blink-and-miss subtleties will alert us (at most) conscious beings. It's crucial to recognize and be wary of inappropriate influences. Understanding power dynamics and identifying how we react to them empowers us to make informed choices. Developing this discernment is essential for navigating decision making effectively in a world filled with manipulation.

When used strategically, AI can leverage vast information—data, context, appropriateness, statistics, and business processes—to predict outcomes, fine-tune interactions, and optimize timing. It is a powerful tool that can adapt to countless scenarios and contribute to success in various environments. AI's role isn't limited to specific tasks; it can support any organization's strategic goals, regardless of industry.

The Architect of Alignment, Your AI Strategist

While the ability of AI to support low-level intelligence domains will not change, its role in contribution will grow from a passive, assistive tool into a strategic partner designed for the alignment and fulfillment of human aspirations. AI's internal organizational assessment could suggest horizontal team reconfigurations or automation of repetitive tasks to have more human capital focus on strategic work. Your AI strategist is the conductor, orchestrating all these parts to play from a shared music sheet. The potential lists of applications are endless and can cross-industry, but the benefits can also be great, from efficiency improvement over productivity gains to groundbreaking innovation. Organizations that harness AI in this succession of opportunities can establish the factors for how well they can respond and thrive in an increasingly digital world. Here are some examples of how AI, as the architect of alignment, can help different industries:

Health Care

- Improving patient care: AI has the potential to study patients' history and health data, hunting for gaps in their treatments that could be corrected through quicker diagnostics and personalized interventions.
- Optimizing resource allocation: AI can predict patient flow, place orders for optimal staffing, and allocate beds more effectively, thus reducing wait times and improving overall patient satisfaction.
- Improving collaboration: AI-enabled communication platforms allow stakeholders to share information, enhancing the synergy among health care professionals and diminishing errors.

Manufacturing

- Predictive maintenance: With access to all the data machines produce and have created, AI can analyze it in real time and predict when something will break before downtime becomes an issue affecting production schedules.
- Quality control: AI vision systems can detect defects on the fly and ensure quality products, reducing waste.
- Supply chain optimization: Using AI, supply change data could be analyzed to point out bottlenecks and inefficiencies, which

would help improve inventory management and, thus, reduce costs.

Retail

- Personalized marketing: AI would process customer data to offer specific promotions or products, elevating consumer engagement and sales.
- Inventory optimization: AI can predict demand and optimize inventory levels to minimize stockout and overstock
- AI chatbots: AI chatbots can be used for customer service automation, removing the burden of handling routine requests from human agents and allowing them to focus on more challenging issues.

Finance

- Fraud detection: AI may examine a transaction and recognize abnormal behavior, helping to detect fraud before it occurs.
- Risk assessment: AI risk bots could use market data to assess risk and better handle your retirement portfolio.
- Onboarding of customers: AI could automate and enrich the process, which leads to faster and error-less onboarding.

Education

- Personalized learning: AI can predict and analyze student data and provide individualized digital learning experiences that improve student engagement and results.
- Administrative automation: One potential use of AI is to automate the routine administrative tasks that take so much time and replace them with a personalized strategy.
- Early intervention: AI might spot students in danger of falling behind and proactively reach out to support them.

Illuminator of Insights: Your AI Oracle

From a data-saturated state, the light-house title of AI Oracle emerges as an active partner sorting through the sea of information to find all these hidden patterns, trends, and correlations that no human would ever see. From assessing social media sentiment to reading the pulse of public opinion, observing minuscule changes in customer behavior, or even running simulations for future event occurrences mimicking market trends—Your AI Oracle gives multiple views and future scenarios of the organizational ecosystem. By gaining expansive insights, leaders can make more informed decisions and reduce risk or take advantage of opportunities with greater confidence. The AI Oracle empowers leaders to see beyond the surface, navigate complexities, and unlock hidden opportunities for growth and success. Here are some examples of how AI, as the illuminator of insights, can help different industries:

Health Care

- Identify disease outbreaks: AI could predict when diseases spread by analyzing public health data, social media trends, and so on. By understanding this in advance, we can take some precautions, like resource allocation and timely interventions, as the skill of prevention is better than cure!
- Identification of Patient Risk Factors: AI can scrutinize far and wide the health history, problems in lifestyle, and even genetic information to determine which patients are at more significant risks for specific diseases, thus leading them toward preventive measures with quite a customized avocation.
- Personalized medicine and drug interactions: AI analyzes large amounts of data for known and emerging interactions in personalized drug predictions. AI can also analyze massive, closed-loop medication data sets with patient outcomes to detect potential safety issues and enhance efficacy.

Manufacturing

- Predictive equipment maintenance: Extending preventative maintenance from the architect of alignment, AI could also evaluate sensor data, service records, and environmental conditions to more effectively predict potential equipment failures before they happen; this proactive approach would reduce downtime.
- Optimizing production process: AI could process production-related data to help identify bottlenecks (hopefully in real-time) and recommend process improvements. This would ultimately increase efficiency, reduce costs, and improve product quality.
- Predicting market trends: AI could predict market trends by analyzing market data flow, consumer behavior, and social media sentiment to anticipate changing customer demand and allow manufacturers to adjust their prices beforehand.

Retail

- Comprehension of consumer taste: AI can learn customer preferences by accurately analyzing purchasing history, browsing activity, and social media feedback in an ad-based marketing campaign.
- Demand prediction: AI can analyze historical sales data, seasonality, and other relevant information to predict how popular specific products will be, resulting in better inventory level optimization with less wasted output.
- Detecting emerging trends: AI could mine social media discussions, online reviews, and fashion blogs to see what is new in demand and upgrade its inventory as customer preferences change.

Finance

- Detection of emerging fraud patterns: AI technologies can leverage transactional and customer behavior data and various external information to detect sophisticated fraud patterns, reducing the cosmological volumes of financial crime.

- Assess market sentiment: AI can analyze news, social media sentiments, and economic data to determine how markets feel, which could help make better investment decisions or risk management strategies.
- Customer exit forecast: As AI learns and records all interactions, historical data like customer transaction history, log information, and demographic details could be used for customer exit predictions. This could further help to save one party or, from another perspective, give a personalized experience.

Education

- At-risk students: AI could help understand if a student is or starts performing poorly, their class records or engagement patterns, and help drive strategies for early exits.
- Predictive models for student success: Utilizing AI to predict academic capability based on vast data feeds, analysis of learning methodologies, and engagement tasks could enable educational institutions to model possible directions students' futures might take and where they need help.
- Adapting curriculum: An AI may analyze student feedback, performance data, and learning outcomes to adapt course materials and teaching specifics for a more tailored experience.

Weaver of Context: Your AI Storyteller

More than data are needed, and context is everything to understand the consequences of information properly. Enter your AI storyteller. Interlacing isolated data threads forms narratives that shed light on the "why" to accompany our quantification of the "what." Let's pretend we have an executive dealing with a legal issue involving many parties. Your AI storyteller can offer brief synopses of relevant case law, pinpoint historical precedence that might unfold similarly, and even extract core points from bulky documents to create a more comprehensive decision-making context. Your AI storyteller transforms data into intelligent information, which will help actionable insights to the leader in a complex situation. Here are some examples of how AI, as the weaver of context, can help different industries:

Health Care

- Patient history summarization: AI can review a patient's medical records, laboratory results, and imaging studies to create a concise summary that can help health care providers with diagnosis and treatment planning.
- Clinical trial narrative creation: AI will analyze data gathered from clinical trials and generate a simple representation of key-sale features and general security profiles with patient experiences. This will position the company to communicate effectively and quickly at any regulatory stage/council (regulatory bodies) so that investors can be interested parties!
- Personal health reports: AI could analyze individual patient data and generate a report that explains the risks of diseases, preventive measures, and treatments—which relies on evidence-based medicine principles to enable patients to make more informed decisions about their chronic conditions.

Manufacturing

- Supply chain risk analysis: AI could analyze supply chain data, news articles, and social media sentiment to infer narratives showing potential risks and disruptions. This could elicit proactive mitigation strategies, thereby sustaining business operations.
- Product performance storytelling: AI could create stories on product performance based on customer feedback, usage data, and warranty claims. These stories would show how well the products worked or identify where they fell short to aid in making future products.
- Employee engagement stories: Identify and tell employee-facing narratives on areas of strength/improvement from the AI analysis performed using various data sources, such as HR

forms, employee surveys, performance reviews, or communication patterns, to better influence HR strategies and maintain a motivated work culture.

Retail

- Customer service: AI analyzes all sorts of customer interactions across various touch points (website visits/social media engagement/in-store purchases) in one giant view whereby, providing an extremely personalized narrative reflecting how this story is narrated at the time with potentially being typically identified as inflection point needing attention.
- Market trend analysis: Another ideal application for AI, market trend analytics could involve the use of algorithms that allow machine learning to process human language; such processing can be used not only to analyze sales data but also competitor activity and ongoing social media conversations in order generate narratives relating to emerging trends or consumer preferences which instead may inform strategies being employed by marketing teams as well with product development.
- Brand reputation monitoring: AI may assess social media sentiment, online reviews, and news to create narratives of brand perception and detect potential reputational risk—managing the narrative instead of reacting.

Finance

- Investment opportunity narratives: AI could analyze all this data, such as market data, company financials, and news sentiment, to produce stories on potential investment opportunities (and risks) by helping investors make more sound decisions.
- Lightening the reporting burden for model risk management (MRM) and compliance: AI could parse through lengthy regulations and internal policies and create plain-English narratives describing what compliance requires for those doing audits, MRM, or even just wanting assurance that their firm

follows legal standards. You can see this in action at Valid-Mind.ai.

- Regulatory financial health assessments: AI would use transaction data, credit history, and so on, and external financial indicators to create narratives of customers.

Education

- Educational resource recommendations: AI can analyze student data about learning styles, interests, and performance to offer personalized education resources and materials that help kids learn independently more efficiently while ensuring they will be interested in the material.
- Student progress reports: AI can review student-level data that include performance, attendance, and learning behavior to produce personalized narratives identifying what students are doing well in, where they need assistance along with suggested activities for improvement, which could be shared via parent communications or used as input into individualized education plans.
- Surveys and assessments: AI analyzes student outcomes, feedback surveys, and assessment data and self-writes narratives that interpret curriculum effectiveness or areas for improvement so we can use an instructional strategy that uses the best evidence available and a story we all find persuasive.
- Educational resource recommendations: AI can analyze student data about learning styles, interests, and performance to offer personalized education resources and materials that help kids learn independently more efficiently while ensuring they will be interested in the material.

Embodiment of Transformation: Your AI Change Agent

A marriage of AI and robotics is at the heart of the game-changing robo-advice tool for your embodiment of transformation, the Change Agent. It is more than automating tasks—from optimizing warehouse logistics to carrying out precision surgeries, reshaping processes, growing capacity, and delivering superior results. Imagine a future where humans and machines work together to unlock never-witnessed-before conclusions, all driven forward by the capabilities provided by AI with moveable parts. Here are some examples of how AI, as the embodiment of transformation, can help different industries:

Health Care

- Surgical robotics: AI-driven surgical robots can help perform complex surgeries, providing high precision, minimal invasiveness, and a looping patient life cycle. Remote surgeries can also be performed, making specialized care available to areas with little access.
- Rehabilitation robots: AI enables the robots to help patients in rehabilitation, create unique exercise protocols according to patient needs, measure progress, and adjust therapy plans according to real-time data.
- Patient monitoring and care: AI-powered robots can observe patients' vitals, dispense medicines, and provide primary care so health professionals can focus on handling more complex activities.

Manufacturing

- Collaborative robots (cobots): AI-driven cobots can work alongside human workers to carry out repetitive or physically demanding tasks, making the process more productive and safe.
- Autonomous vehicles: AI-driven autonomous vehicles can transport materials and goods around warehouses and factories, streamlining logistics and lowering labor costs.
- Inspection robots: AI-powered robots with advanced sensors and vision systems for detailed quality inspections to keep the product consistent with minimal defects.

Retail

- Inventory management robots: AI-powered robots can help businesses establish an automated inventory system that tracks the overall quantity and low-level item reordering.
- Customer service robots: AI-integrated robots are adept at customer interaction, can provide product information, and even guide them through the purchase process.
- Delivery robots: AI-controlled robots can be set loose to deliver packages and groceries to customers' homes, providing a convenient and efficient delivery system for food ordered from grocery stores or weekly diets.

Finance

- Robo-advisors: AI-based robo-advisors offer customized investment advice, execute automated trading, and trade on behalf of the client, making financial planning less expensive and more accessible.
- Trading bots: Utilizing AI trading bots that process trades rapidly, market data analysis, and the ability to locate profitable commercial opportunities may increase return on investment (ROI) results with less associated risk.
- Customer onboarding and support robots: AI-driven robots help with customer onboarding, questions, and support, leading to faster response times.

Education

- Educational robots: AI-enabled robots can communicate, tutor, and modify their teaching methods according to each student's learning style, increasing their involvement in academics and achievement.
- Administrative robots: Admins tend to evolve as the enablers, with AI-driven robots taking over tasks like grading assignments or keeping track of attendance and schedule, and so on, letting educators focus more on teaching itself and student interaction.

- Research and data analyzing robots: AI robots can help research-
  ers collect and analyze data and test hypotheses, speeding up
  scientific discoveries and innovations.

The organizational benefit of influencing through AI is resourceful
in varied dimensions. Together, these AI superpowers, the Strategist,
Oracle, Storyteller, and Change Agent, aim to unlock their potential
for organizations to accelerate innovation and growth. Where AI is
heading in the future: Not just automation but collaboration, insights,
and transformation. That information can position your company for
strategic success, give you foresight by identifying hidden patterns and
simulating outcomes, help clarify confusing data so decisions are made
quickly and accurately—and even empower robots to take actions in
the physical world. By intentionally utilizing AI as a strategist, oracle,
storyteller, and change agent, you unlock unprecedented capabilities
to influence your surroundings for the better—and deliver superior
performance.

AI-Fueled Roadmaps: Navigating the Future With Confidence

In a world where organizations are becoming more data-driven, a
roadmap might be necessary to help guide the programs and initiatives
that must drive those strategies. Few remember the power of patience
and timing in business roadmaps. By considering where AI fits into your
broader roadmap, you can ensure that you allocate time and budget to
projects with the most potential ROI.

As a massive fan of roadmaps at the organizational level and an
individual workgroup's evolution, pinning things down and affirming
delivery is essential in getting us from where we are now to the future
destination. A powerful vision that is, unfortunately, somewhat fixed.
Execution is the realm where so much can go wrong with well-intentioned planning. The bottom line to integrating AI initiatives with your
current roadmap and obtaining executive buy-in comes in several forms:

Identify areas of interest and window for opportunity: What insights would give a material edge to the AOIs of the current plan? Find processes ready for disruption, decision points needing support, or enhancements to support experiences.

Assess feasibility and priority: Ensure you have the data, resources, and capability to act on insights from the proposed AI-driven processes. An excellent recommendation is only helpful if it can be put into practice. Balance AI initiatives against your other roadmap items. Measure them by their potential value, the degree of alignment with your goals, and the level of effort. This allows you to determine the most efficient way of distributing resources.

Refactor your roadmap: Stay ready to pivot your path. The now-added AI initiatives may uncover new opportunities or unmet needs in your initial plans and can expose insight into the potential weakness of your original intentions. Be open to how AI can influence and shape your strategy for the better.

Establishing Influential Scope

Our view of "scope" is routinely predefined by the immediate imperative, yet it does not carry through the widespread mechanism-transformation-centered perspectives needed to reimagine process, procedure, and interaction. Typical "scope" involves well-intended work efforts that yield appropriate solutions. Sadly, it's just not enough. If you can interact with an audience, why not enrich the interaction by asking in an influential way?

Scoping influence is mapping a journey with strategically placed guidance. A simple trick to influential power is to focus on executing one thing—what are you going after above all else? Clear goals make it easier to keep your AI initiatives on course. Zoom in and out of your area of interest, understanding one thing that can make a tremendous difference. Then, start to pull out timelines, sequences, and interactions concerning knowing how these processes interfaced with one another and recognizing critical deadlines. To dig deeper, use investigative tools and AI to identify bottlenecks and streamline your processes.

Unveiling the Landscape and Pinpointing Opportunities

While strategic scoping is often considered a preliminary step, it catalyzes sweeping organizational change. It goes beyond merely setting project boundaries to develop a full-fledged roadmap that paints a picture of our journey and enables organizations to know how best to achieve successful AI integration.

Strategic scoping within AOIs is fundamentally about developing an intimate understanding of what makes your organization unique and where it aspires to be. To create a panoramic view of the landscape and deploy AI strategically across specific areas, you must ask questions about your goals, operational context, and timelines. Empowered with your influential road map, begin identifying high-impact AI levers:

Analysis points: Where do things bottleneck? Where data are the most plentiful (or helpful in identifying any shockingly empty spots), and the AI program is well suited to find patterns for breakthroughs.

Influence points: Breaking down where AI-powered insights can have the most influence. Look for decision points, bottlenecks, or areas where guided AI can be the most beneficial. Influence points help focus the moments when AI can have a transformative impact and bolster the human ability to make decisions more effectively—and on the kind of innovation we aspire to.

Timing: Timing is everything with influence, and the point of analysis may be far away from the point of influence, both in physical proximity and time. Make sure your AI implementation plan is complete. Remembering the deadlines, anticipating delays, and having a plan B are vital. It is now time to get AI-powered and integrated.

Embrace the possibilities and implement them into your business at strategic points to access a new level of efficiency, productivity, and innovation that will help propel you further toward sustained success in the days ahead. Transitioning from analysis to action enables you to get out of the investigative mode and proactively do something about what is happening in your business. By linking AI's transformative capabilities to your organization's specific needs, you can generate results that enable scale and performance you have never seen before. AI as a Partner, not just a tool, can:

Empower and augment existing workflows: Allow people to leave their monotonous routines and do other things at a higher level.

Reveal anomalies and outliers: Conduct analyses to bring hidden insights from massive data sets and gain the ability to see patterns and trends to create analytics-driven decisions/innovations.

Optimize and streamline: Make your workflows, communication, and collaboration more agile and efficient.

Establishing organizational participation: AI can only succeed in supporting organizational aspirations through supportive and collaborative human expertise.

Using your team's creativity and experience to enhance AI's capabilities is required. It is also how you make it personal and let it find patterns you had not considered. Recognition of the importance your workforce plays in the advancement of the organization lifts spirits and leads to the adoption of AI. Not to mention, the extensive viewpoints that come from workforce involvement can help protect AI against unintended consequences. Conversely, employees must be aligned with AI goals and objectives, which may worsen matters. Consistent communication, such as monthly reporting or regular meetings, keeps everyone in the loop and on track with organizational goals. Open communication fosters progress—admitting errors encourages experimentation, and many new possibilities can be uncovered.

Organizations like Domino's (DPZ) are taking an on-the-ground approach. The test kitchen is a group of team members from different company parts working in a real, live kitchen. Benefits can be pretty juicy for immersion, including but not limited to:

Empathy, a changed role, and better decisions: Without the rubber hitting the road on those traditional duties, team members can experience walking in front-line employees' shoes, leading to more informed decisions.

Action: Being in the process allows each team member to
see bottlenecks (inefficient processes, communication gaps, or
technology that doesn't support the current workflow).

Matching realities: In the test kitchen, Domino's corporate team
learns how seemingly simple Headquarters decisions can impact
and affect day-to-day actions.

New ideas: From the outside, hands-on feedback can provide a
fresh perspective on how to be more productive, deliver better
customer service, or improve food taste.

While Domino's has undoubtedly paved the way, this model is not
reserved solely or primarily for food. Here are a couple more ways how
you can help teach about operations concepts:

Job shadowing: Matching people from different departments with
frontline workers.

Interactive rotations: Participate in and understand the pain points
of audience interactions.

Field visits: Visit the organization's offices, branches, stores, and
facilities to gain insights, see the process, and experience the flow.

Immersion programs build a more cohesive customer-centric culture
together. Employees have more skin in the game, leading to better
decision making, efficiency, and higher profits because everyone is vested
in the organization's success. In support of accumulating knowledge
from all experiences, a comprehensive, linked decision repository keeps
your decisions (and the information on which they were based) in
context—it is a living map of assets, data flows, experimental scenario
results, and variable factors that affect how your business operates.
It enables good choices by capturing current conditions to underline
adaptiveness.

Cultivating Knowledge for Organizational Artificial Thinking

Championing operational automation, integrating external insights,
and utilizing influence tactics in concert allows organizations to reach
astonishing heights that enable them to navigate complex scenarios with

strategic human-like judgment. However, behaviors must be nurtured in this fluid future to create an educated and invested workforce. While ongoing monitoring is essential, it's also necessary to provide the team with a sense of how they will be altered and allow them to change strategies so that they are not sitting on their laurels.

AI implementation needs to work on risk, control, and ethics. MRM has predominantly focused on validating banking models. With AI playing a more significant part in enterprise decision making moving forward, MRM needs to be more than these diminutive roles; it needs to grow into an integrated strategic function within organizations. This evolution requires extending the scope of MRM, reflecting how distributed decisions and corresponding influence are organized within the organization. It would be best to map these AI-driven insights and actions as they move throughout an organization, impacting decision making at every level. Your officially appointed influence architect owns and manages the complex web of influence, including but not limited to the delivery and impact of AI-driven insights to align with broad goals, organizational consciousness, and ethical deliberations.

Expanding MRM functions with increasing contextual understanding and providing an all-encompassing categorization system for AI efforts in three critical high-level categories: influential AI, investigative AI, and alignment AI. These categories, however simple, help designate usage and, as we will see later in this book, align further with a flexible information management strategy. In regards to additional MRM functions, it is worth expanding deeper and sharing directly with the line of business team members on:

> Business and model scope: Provide expanded details on the specific business problem your model solves, what team it is owned by (the business team), how it impacts the team's work functions, and a mapping of how it addresses a business goal along with what's to be done when the AI is not working.
> Data scope and freshness: Expanded documentation of the flows supporting data collection for transparency and traceability. Ensure data are regularly checked for relevance to keep decision making accurate and reliable.

Expected decision/usage pattern: Describe how model outputs will be used and integrated into workflow decisions, further defining and establishing traceability for AI's place in achieving business objectives.

Audience and exposure: Beyond the workers, who is the audience impacted by this model (internally or externally), and what would responsible use look like? Are there particular audiences and contexts that are not supported? What happens downstream if an audience is exposed to the model?

Expected lifespan: Ascertain the extent to which your model should live. Calculate your model's expected lifespan based on the data's relevance, usefulness across processes, and decay value so you can know when it needs an update or replacement.

Comparative perspectives: Contrast the model focus with extant models to gauge what may overlap, not cover, or synergistic for a more comprehensive problem-solving orientation. What role is your model playing in the larger choice-making structure? This offers a great commission to discuss what exactly you have trained for and how that should translate into more meaningful requirements—as dependent on a closer affinity of this position, type of decision logic, and expected contribution (in absolute terms) back toward pushing up bottom-line parameters.

Contextual alignment: Restate and align the business question to the context essential, maintaining laser focus; represent the current context and how it (and related assumptions) might change so that we can continue to make the model's outputs applicable and adaptable over time. Transparency breeds trust, mainly because it helps ensure that users and stakeholders understand what the model can do—and, just as importantly, what it cannot. Also, document how the model may not fit a shift in the context.

Weight of business decision: We must understand how impactful the decision is relative to other aspects so we can incorporate it or include/exclude this dimension in our risk assessment process.

Expanding MRM to include a more detailed segmentation and contextualization will allow companies to invest in managing influence and risks. The influence architect and the MRM team ensure alignment by controlling the distribution of AI-informed insights to meet business needs while maintaining responsible/ethical use and deploying for top organizational outcomes. AI integration is not about technology, per se; it's a matter of controlling and focalizing AI's influence to make the organization more intelligent or adaptive.

AI as a Motionless Means of Interaction

A "motionless means" seems a farfetched idea in an always-on, changing-at-the-speed-of-light universe. An end goal signals a frictionless state of proactive alignment—influences take place so far upstream that the impact barely registers; it's more of a guiding whisper than a dynamic push. It is like making a course correction five miles in advance, enabling a smooth and lean way to reach the intended destination.

If I had to describe a modern experience resembling this, it would be the cars' lane departure warning feature. Auto lane return, which automatically nudges the vehicle back into its lane if it begins to wander, could avoid a potential accident before one occurs. Aside from the alerts, as a supportive nudge, the driver will most likely not be aware of the correction taking place—a real-world example of Influence at a fundamental level to providing a safer and more comfortable ride.

As skillful as the finest artwork, implementing AI nudges means you understand the dynamics of your system well; you can foresee misalignments upstream and deal with subtle changes that will have gigantic impacts downstream. But it's a way of operating that is proactive rather than reactive and strategic in effect (i.e., the right balance between unpredictability and dependency).

The art of unlocking the transformational promise of a motionless means of interaction is an extensive proactive alignment that subtly steers desired outcomes. Alignment enhances efficiencies, nourishes maximum impact, and allows for extended innovation. Before you can effectively integrate AI into your workforce, see the integration and mapping of your AI technologies and applications. Create explicit diagrams or flowcharts indicating the path of the data, forms, and decision points where errors/misuse can happen. Share this information with everyone in your organization to create transparency and incentivize collaboration.

Because transparency is a trust-building component, educate your team on the foundations of AI systems and their operation. Create training for them on how to read AI output and identify patterns and areas where they could collaborate. Urge transparent communication and feedback around AI efforts. Interact with and work upon the feedback and suggestions you receive to show the people about whom you are building it; their inputs matter so that the system can be refined, which further helps improve your AI work. To strengthen the collaboration between human and AI workforces, implement these fundamental mechanisms within your influence workflow:

Know your baselines: Yes, "baselines" is plural. Research your target interactions and audiences to learn how they behave and what other internal or broader circumstances may also inform their decisions, laying the groundwork for powerful influence strategies.

Prepare for and think in terms of motion: Anticipate all elements in motion and predict multiple outcome scenarios, thus understanding the best locations, positions, and timings for setting up suitable guardrails.

Orchestrate interactions: Create tiny, discreet, and motionless interactions that enrich experiences and nudge behavior toward the best path and desired outcomes.

Finetune for balance: Consider the eventual effect of influence and try to maximize the sustainable gain versus the short-term win. Keep an eye on diminishing returns and be agile; behavior shifts can lead to patterns not previously recognized.

Leverage Organizational Flow for Motionless Influence

Influence architects look for points of influence to make quiet, disruptive nudges, and in doing so, they can discern "still points of interaction" and hence more effectively (and efficiently) leverage movements for long-term benefit. A set of three guiding principles helps support a long-term focus on influence:

Swift adoption: Ideally, your audience can quickly embrace new practices and tech to keep up with the competition. Influence architects to drive forward supportive communication, remove concerns, and change alignment with current workflows. They reduce resistance with little disruption associated with change and, perhaps most importantly, positive emphasis.

Nourish utilization and relevance: Cementing the need for a new practice or technology is a starting point that requires regular communication, ongoing training, feedback with results, and delivering positive outcomes. Influence architects are responsible for building these elements into the organizational culture and including them in everyday operations.

Managing de-adoption: Organizations must face the fact that as they evolve, sometimes even the most effective practices, processes, or technologies will need to be sunset. Influence architects are crucial to facilitating de-adoption, tempering resistance during the phasing out of these platforms, offering alternatives, and responding to concerns. Through strategic de-adoption, they keep the ship steady as new initiatives arise.

Only in the context of the unique organization and type of change will Architects be able to apply concepts successfully. They will know intimately what organizations do day-to-day and how they think, acting with foresight about where implementation might create turbulence. They will know when to speed up, on the other hand, when to back off and tailor their process for those specific conditions. Influence architects can find tiny leverage points in the flow of organizational events and use them to set up cascades with a substantial long-term effect. This way, change is more readily accepted and adopted aggressively, making the environment more robust yet dynamic. Best of all, successful influence requires harnessing brief yet powerful "nonkinetic means." These may come in different shapes and sizes and be adjusted for context or purpose. So, how can AI help? Here are several examples:

Information-based insights: AI is beneficial for analyzing large data sets to bulge out hidden patterns and information, which can help make better decisions. Presented succinctly, these insights can subtly guide the organization to one particular end or another on a continuum—essentially, what influences architects do.

Personalized communication: AI-driven tools can study individual communication styles and preferences to create messages that are most likely to appeal (for example), leading to increased interest and interaction with the individuals getting your message.

Behavioral nudges: AI can form sneaky prods, such as reminders, to motivate the performance of desired behaviors. In the above example, a fitness tracker can send tailored alerts based on knowing how you are regularly at home and encourage you to keep moving. It's a very different context, encouragement for a new routine, than "tracking" workouts.

Environmental augmentation: AI could tune the physical or digital environment to alter mood and intentions. They might change the lighting, play music, or showcase specific visuals to set a particular mood auto-magically.

Precision fit: AI can provide scarily accurate individual-specific personalization. For example, your coffee machine might be able to remember how strong you like it or what temperature and serve you a consistently perfect cup.

Situational support: AI alerts and reminders help individual contributors and teams remain informed. They combine real-time data with trending signals to prompt proactive action by surfacing potential risks, identifying opportunities, or reminding people about deadlines.

Sequential framing: Use AI to frame information and interactions sequentially for the best long-term impact. AI can learn individual learning styles and preferences to provide more appealing information and experiences.

Artificial human extensions: Artificial human extensions focus on AI directly aligning with human biology. The goal is not just to create intelligent machines but also to augment and implement our capabilities in a way that allows excellent synergy of AI and biological systems, from AI-powered prosthetics providing an unprecedented amount of control and movement that looks natural, to sensory augmentation which will enhance not only our auditory sense but visual perception beyond what has previously been possible. For example, brain–computer interfaces can introduce thought-controlled devices and direct brain communication, while AI-driven personalized medicine could revolutionize health care with treatments personal to everyone.

Influence architects bridge this gap by utilizing AI wisely to empower best practices and a continuous improvement and innovation culture while developing alignment within and with external stakeholders. This results in a peaceful environment; AI becomes a natural, closer part of human workflows that can help each other to be best and add the most successful growth into the organization. This subtle but powerful influence enables sustained behavior change without the need to be loud or pushy.

Influence is potent in driving decisions, motivating action, and moving mountains. With human values as a guide, we have an unprecedented chance in the age of AI to use established insight into how minds are changed and decide what tactics represent best practices for influencing this technology. Social psychology expert Robert Cialdini's "Seven Principles of Persuasion" is essential reading, as it establishes an explicit syntax for thinking through and applying these principles in an evolving AI environment:[22]

1. Reciprocity: Reciprocity, the act of giving something to get something in return, is how AI analyzes user behavior and preferences to provide highly personalized rewards or incentives that feel naturally integrated. Consider a language learning app that gives users one free lesson for the topic they have expressed interest in, creating an exposure to gratefulness and reciprocity-in-the-making that encourages further user engagement.

2. Commitment/consistency: Commitment/consistency highlights how people want their beliefs to be consistent with their values. Chatbots can use AI technology to maintain a natural conversation flow by changing prompts according to the user's feedback. It allows for slight commitment escalation that leads the users to want actions still playing in their heads. For instance, an advisor chatbot could begin by asking about saving behavior and eventually steer the users toward automatic contributions for a retirement account.

3. Social proof: Social proof supports being validated by what others are doing. To help audience validation, AI algorithms can display social proofing—messages that resonate most soundly with individual segments—to signal the value of a path to users. Social media platforms already play off of trending topics or what the user's friends or demographic are into—that is, using others to say it's good so more will follow (social validation).

4. Authority: Supporting human nature and obeying authority figures, AI can pull from an array of authoritative sources and signals in a way that flows with the context at hand and user profile. For example, a medical AI chatbot might refer to key research papers or expert opinions on the user's health areas it aligns with, which is conducive to building trust.

5. Engagement and liking: If you like someone or something, you are more likely to be influenced by it. AI-led personalization enables lifelong learning from every user interaction, such as how to build rapport or affinity through always-on dynamic matching of content types and suggestions. In the digital space, AI can be similar to a personal stylist, assuming more about what to recommend each time you provide feedback so that its suggestions become highly personalized and engaging.

6. Real-time scarcity: AI can analyze data in real-time to understand if a product is running low on stock, what the demand for that item looks like, or which offers are timed and provide immediate insights. For example, a travel booking website can use AI to identify user decision-making pauses. It may display

last-minute offers or signal growing unavailability for great deals on travel packages.

7. Unity: AI can be used to examine shared themes in data that uncover common identities, personalize communications to highlight oneness, and develop a sense of belonging through shared experiences—we are members of the same group.

Integrating AI with the well-researched principles of persuasion can be a powerful strategy for organizations to influence people and behaviors while building trust. In short, we can enable the best of both worlds—human judgment superpowers powered by AI capabilities—to unleash greater productivity and innovation for transformation at scale.

Ripple Effects: The Unintended Consequences of AI Influence

While influence is a powerful tool, achieving the desired outcome is more complex. Every action, especially with AI-driven influence, can create unintended consequences beyond the initial target. Recognizing this reality and actively anticipating ripple effects is essential. Only then can organizations harness the full potential of their AI investments and ensure sustainable and responsible influence management across their entire ecosystem.

To truly understand and manage these ripple effects, we need to delve deeper into the context surrounding each action and the motivations driving it. For example, a seemingly successful marketing campaign might boost sales in the short term, but it could also inadvertently alienate a specific customer segment or trigger a competitor's aggressive response. Understanding ripple effects allows organizations to proactively address long-term sustainable growth rather than short-term gains at the expense of future stability. Adopting a long-term perspective over short-term wins with AI's influence maximizes benefits and mitigates risks for several reasons:

Maximizing benefits: By anticipating and managing ripple effects, organizations can ensure their AI initiatives generate sustained positive outcomes, not just fleeting successes.

Mitigate risks: A long-term view allows for proactive risk management, identifying and addressing potential pitfalls before they escalate into major problems.

Uncover opportunities: Organizations can discover and capitalize on unexpected market opportunities by closely monitoring the ripple effects of actions.

Both the good and the bad come in ripples. It is essential to anticipate and control them, not only your ripple but also those of others. By understanding larger contexts and playing fields, it is possible to collectively deploy a more strategic approach that could make a more significant difference. Shaping the narrative of AI influence is an intricate terrain that requires a solid understanding of these impacts and contributions to long-term, sustainable strategies. iPhones are great examples; initial success in creating demand led to a change in consumer behavior, something Apple had orchestrated brilliantly. Recently, Apple moved away from reporting unit sales as the annual or semiannual refresh no longer swayed consumers.[23] A simple question, "Do I need the new features?" reflected a shift in consumer thinking, not a rejection of the product itself. The change in pricing, from free phones to financing plans, also prompted a re-evaluation of the constant upgrade cycle.

Influence is seldom a straight line; it's an intricate network of interactions. Anything you do can have a long and far-reaching influence on your audience, the market, or even your company. By being forward-thinking and adaptable, you are well-equipped to maneuver through this landscape fluidly and take full advantage of the transforming abilities of AI. Misaligned efforts can have far-reaching repercussions. The last thing you would want after deciding to provide a discount is for call agents to surprise customers who did not receive the same discount with angry calls. That could result in unhappy customers and, therefore, a public relations (PR) nightmare.

Versioning the Future

Simulation and scenario planning allow organizations to visualize the future and imagine possible consequences beyond immediate impacts, including models for predicting ecosystem responses to the future. What if scenarios offer more than proof that things can turn out differently based on factors? This notion of the same "what if" also has application in teaching you how to create an outcome or, even more so, as a guide for what action should occur when things do not go correctly. Assume that success is not a state but a flow. Delve into the nuances besides your key metrics. Are customers speaking in fresh ways on social? How are your competitor's pricing? Are you worried about your team's morale? The more significant changes are these early warning signs.

"Nurture" is not a control freak but the influence architect of your organization, working with the leadership who is well aware of micro and macro scenarios in your sector and can navigate through turbulent and unknown conditions. As a seasoned captain might, this expert guides you through the pitfalls and vagaries of change and where compelling uncertainty often brings opportunity. Agility at this level cannot be achieved without a well-informed, empowered, and engaged workforce inspired by the influence architect who stands at the intersection of your workforce and machineforce.

Empowering the AI-Driven Workforce

A recent KPMG survey confirms that generative AI is having a growing impact on workforce productivity and is expected to alter how people work and foster innovation significantly.[25] Thanks to consumer electronics, employees are ready for the change and need guidance. While the potential of AI, robotics, and automation is undeniable, the question of control remains. How can businesses effectively integrate intelligent technologies while maintaining stability, empowering the workforce, and minimizing disruption?

Take a minute and promote yourself to the CEO of a midsize company. Turning your company's future over to AI—no matter how advanced—is scary. While leading as the CEO, you see the need to innovate. That said, you're most likely reluctant to give up control. Such hesitation often results in an unnecessarily risk-averse, tentative strategy toward AI projects that grants permission only to the "safest."

Employees already have AI on their phones, in their houses, and in their vehicles. Get past the hesitation, become more flexible, and give AI tools to your employees! Demonstrate trust in their abilities and help them closely monitor activities to protect the company. It's not about "democratizing AI" but rather empowering employees with a structure on how to wield a powerful tool's influence. Give team members a "license to experiment" under supervision—an idea extensively supported by the *Harvard Business Review*'s "Creating a Culture of Experimentation."[24] A culture of experimentation promotes the safe use of AI and educates the workforce. Some ideas will work while others won't, and the experimentation phase will mitigate damage from incorrect paths, a positive mode that enables innovation with no reduction of stability for the company. Ensure the workforce understands that experimentation in a sandbox is safe; employees can take risks, learn from their mistakes, and innovate. An atmosphere that promotes curiosity and creativity, fundamentals to popularizing optimistic AI across the organization. It can also be a way to combat some of the concerns over too democratic, unmonitored AI models.

Remember that your veteran employees are professionals in the organization, well beyond their professions; they know your business processes intimately. Engaging the organization's internal team to see how fun discoveries can be made will lead people to get hands-on with AI and experimentation, fostering a sense of excitement and engagement.

The Influence Architect: Guiding AI Adoption

AI adoption at this scale is more than just a technological implementation. It's a journey through uncharted waters, navigating uncertainty and aligning complex systems. As the landscape becomes increasingly complex, leaders need guidance and a strategic vision. This is where the influence architect comes in, aligning all aspects of AI integration with the strategic priorities of executive decision makers. Much like a masterful navigator using the stars to create an archetypal "map of paint" for your company, the influence architect builds this map. This shows the intricate balance between teams, AI systems, and strategic goals through a map with different harmonious areas and continuously conflicting back-to-business decision making. As such, this is not a reactive tool enabling you to address issues that have already turned into significant roadblocks—instead, you can use it proactively for course correction and anticipate and address any potential challenges.

The influence architect offers technical understanding and a strategic vision rarely seen together. They know how to communicate AI results in simple terms and convert them into easy-to-understand insights for the executives. They also provide the rallying cry to unite teams around a shared vision and make sure that AI efforts have purposeful alignment with the overarching organizational strategy.

Imagine an AI-based churn model created with advanced technology that still loses its spark to drive down customer attrition. Beyond the model, an influence architect could see misaligned goals between sales and marketing teams, resulting in conflicting customer engagement strategies. With this in mind, leadership has clarity and can act decisively to realign key performance indicators (KPIs).

Alignment brings a newly optimized AI model with extended influence points to drive improved organizational integration and a better ROI. The influence architect supports tracking, managing, and maximizing the **return on AI** (RoAI). A key indicator of AI adoption that provides reassurance and confidence to the entire organization. As a part of RoAI, influence architects:

Identify and address root cause: They don't just treat symptoms; they uncover and tackle deeper systemic, often nontechnical, problems across organizational boundaries that inhibit AI project success.

Align cross-functional teams: They can break down silos and encourage cross-functional cooperation and competition, along with ensuring efforts are consistent with corporate strategy.

Empower leadership: Influence architect breaks down complex processes and corresponding AI into clear, actionable recommendations for leaders to make decisions that drive real impact.

Embracing Disaggregation: The Hidden Costs of Over Consolidation

Throughout history, our approach to data has revolved around aggregation. Data are rolled up, metrics are aggregated, and summaries are sought to view from a higher level. While valuable, the analysis is only helpful in assessing high-level macro trends. The simple act of aggregating data can remove meaningful contexts, rendering employees without the granular knowledge to enable real-time decisions, and is further complicated in highly dynamic organizations.

Turning the data service model dial again may require a shift in strategy toward disaggregation to steer through ever-changing environments. It is not a complete stop; it means interacting with data at an atomic level and a consolidated perspective. By directly exploring individual data points that are related in some way, we can better understand what trends and anomalies may be hidden behind the aggregated view. The richness of information makes us more precise and accurate in our decision making—with the hopes of improving results. Here's some additional details on why it matters:

Context is king: Look closely at the details of disaggregated data as high-level summaries hide significant information. Operations can understand what drives actual world outcomes; employees can provide process knowledge to help uncover subtleties, odd scenarios, and hidden relationships that tend to define the larger picture.

Adapting to change: In rapidly changing contexts, disaggregated insights expose slight transitions that may serve as early signals of seismic disruption or potential gains. By recognizing early, there's time to adjust and prevent the cascading consequences from out-of-date aggregates.

Empowered decision making: With granular data, agile teams can make informed decisions (without waiting for top-down directives formed on summarized reports) and quickly test possible solutions without needing development help. This, in turn, improves organizational agility and creates an ownership culture.

Disaggregation can be complex, but this granularity becomes an invaluable resource for organizations with a solid data management practice. Leaders build an authentic data-informed culture by empowering teams to dive into the data granularly and from a bird's-eye view. This transition enables organizations to be more predictive, drive innovation, and operate effectively in a volatile ecosystem. When harnessing AI for invisible dynamics, balance all the perspectives and vantage points between the details and the big picture!

CHAPTER 5

Fluxive Leadership

The Illusion of Unbounded Perception

It's not about the destination—the intentional actions taken during the journey shape the outcome.

Given perspective and limitations, humans receive information and instinctively know how something may seem or feel. Despite the sophistication of human cognition, our perception is fundamentally limited. Some may argue the finer points of these constraints, philosophically speaking at least, but we can all agree that they are lived as a physical certainty. For our sake and the growth of our organization, continuous learning is essential to adapt appropriately. As a part of our learning, we should always remember that there are several built-in constraints to our perception. Furthermore, it is vital to acknowledge the system's constraints when we frame situations and deploy AI to influence. Some of how our perception gets limited include:

Physical limitations: Our senses have limitations. We see only a
small range of light, hear a narrow portion of sound frequencies,
and so on.
Cognitive constraints: Given that no one has the time in their day,
let alone the space of mind, to keep track of all this data our
senses pick up—we filter.
Biases and assumptions: The world appears the way it does to
each individual because we interpret our experiences through a
particular belief system.

The unknown unknowns: There are things we need to realize that
you recognize, the substantial parts of fact beyond our present
understanding.

Absence of environmental awareness: Imagine a measuring tape:
its measurements are arbitrary, a human-created reference for
working together. For example, something could be one inch to
one person, becoming 2.54 centimeters in another perspective.

Human perception and awareness can sometimes trick us into
thinking we have a boundless perspective of the universe—a view of
our lives as we experience them efficiently and objectively. Despite this,
we tend to forget that our view is limited at the core—and costly.

Recognizing our limitations can help us to understand what this era
of rapid change means in terms of the evolution of modern leadership—
oversight bridging a human workforce and an artificially intelligent
machineforce.

In the modern, fast-paced world, leadership must deal with an
overabundance of information from different sources and from people
with and without immediate experience. When flooded with abundant
information, increased thinking paces, and shorter attention spans, you
must pivot quickly and attune your strategy, continuing to be a leader
instead of a boss. "One thing that distinguishes a boss from a leader is
the ability to suspend belief and disbelief so that innovations and new
processes will have a chance to emerge."[19]

In support of suspending belief, fluxive leadership offers a simple psychological framework for quickly operating within uncertainty,
changing, and re-establishing yourself. Fluxive leaders know that
direction changes—typically on time scales of minutes or seconds,
sometimes going to days, weeks, and months, sometimes years. As
situational leaders, they comprehensively understand the intricate
ecosystem inside and outside the organization, with an extended range
beyond individual tasks or projects. Today's tactic might not make sense
for tomorrow but with a view to the long-term vision in mind.

Being a fluxive leader goes beyond simply being flexible. It is
about making dynamism a life-long leadership principle and not just
something to get through in your next career transition. Our world

changes so quickly with technology that new AI features can upend entire industries over distances of a year or two. The old ideas are out the window alone. At the heart of what we believe are to be accurate opinions based on decades of real-life practice, proper leadership adaptability looks something like this:

Increasing contextual awareness: Examine decisions in and of themselves, consider them from various sides, and consider the entire organizational ecology.

Prioritizing agility: Creating a fabric and architecture to respond rapidly to unexpected shifts.

Embracing experimentation: Compelled risk-taking and personal responsibility failures.

Creating a growth mindset: I constantly seek to learn and change skills to maintain skill sets on par with the transformation happening around us.

Empowering others: Adaptable team, learning, and flexible teams

Optimizing AI beyond automation: Leveraging the pervasive impact of AI to enhance environments and streamline processes that create the illusion of "motionless" interactions about successful results.

Strategic positioning and patience: The crucial ability is the extraordinary patience and restraint to catch a natural sailing wind, not quick breezes that may send you off course or toward an overpriced energy sucker with decreasing marginal returns. But paying attention to the calm…. The break before a storm, pausing strategically amid comfort and ease for reflection and preparation that can leverage your emerging peak state, helps this stillness turn into stiller waters.

Influence: Fluxive leaders are influential leaders who do not believe they are in control; instead, they welcome change as their truth, which helps them find confidence and strength amidst the shifts.

By embracing fluxive leadership as your flexible mindset and methodology, leaders survive and thrive on change. They create opportunities left, right, and center, range themselves to catch these winds of transformation, and ride them higher. In this era of AI, and in a world where a machineforce follows, we have never needed fluxive leadership more.

Radical Transformation: Reimagining Work With AI

With AI's promises for growth and technology's exponential potential, it is no wonder there are complications when scaling the organization comes into play. Technology will play a significant role, but organizations must understand their internal flow. To capitalize on the flow, we need to motivate employees toward peak cross-functional productivity and, in return, provide them with financial gain, recognition, and even ownership stakes. Even with technology playing a significant role, disruption will occur. One thing is sure: old metrics will not suffice, and leaders must move beyond managing siloed, fragmented data and individual teams and adopt an extended process-based view. In the interest of being fluxive, it means being willing to step into a more flexible and influential position by letting go of the need for complete control.

Many of the most critical workflows, steps, and resources are often invisible to those higher-ups because they exist outside formal systems. The lack of visibility becomes even more problematic in a fast-changing scenario, where traditional metrics can seem outdated after only a minute. Now is the time to confront the organization's old habits, close out old systems, scrutinize what's taken for granted, and search for fresh perspectives. Traditional metrics need to be replaced by innovative insights that can offer fresh, comprehensive views of our organizations. The winners of the future are those who can adjust to these shifting sands and make change their friend (or at least companion). Here are some elements to keep in mind:

Working on unsteady ground:
If we face reality, perfect baselines remain a fair tale of folklore.
Organizations are not controlled lab experiments; they live in the messy real world.

Background Noise:

This could be a competitor, the economy, or even your data getting
in its way — making it challenging to say what is causing change
because of one thing you changed! When do we misinterpret
the signal for noise? If you cannot put something in context, it
is essentially background noise and someone else's or something
else's context.

Hidden Factors:

You may need to document your company's operational activities.
You cannot decide that you have fixed things if your workplace's baseline is so low and shaky. Of course, hidden figures are
everything that we should pay attention to.

Surprise Wins:

Sometimes, the best things happen when we embrace the unexpected and allow external factors to shape our paths.

If the objective constantly moves, how do you know when you
win? Fortunately, we can adopt a new iterative development and growth
paradigm mirroring today's business. If you're unprepared, tap into your

Figure 5.1 Orienting and acting, a fluxive dance

organization for information. Talk to your employees and customers and see how the changes impact them. Empathize—go through the process yourself. It is important to note that adaptability counts! Some things demand changing with them. Collect data and iterate your process. It's as simple as that! By combining data and a desire to improve, you can monitor your progress on the way forward. It is more akin to a man leading his dancing partner, where the music that plays guides both, each from time to time having an opportunity to lead and follow (Figure 5.1).

The Fluxive Leadership Model: Embracing the Infinite Loop of Adaptation

Fluxive leadership isn't a starched, stuck linear line path; it's an active, dynamic dance with change. You can look at it in two ways: first, identify the opportunities that change brings and then normalize steps to extract more from them. Think of someone who can navigate a small boat in the middle of an ocean. They recheck their position, align the sails, and confirm they are still heading in the right direction for what is true north. One second, they slog vigorously; the other moment, they muse over things, stopping to investigate moving frequencies and resetting a course. This episodic cycle of focusing and acting is the crux of fluxive leadership and is dynamic enough for modern needs. Change is not a barrier but an integral part of progress, providing occasions for self-expansion and adjustment. Fluxive leadership is, in its very nature, cyclical.

As a simple two-sided cycle of orientation and action, fluxive leadership strategically places a dynamic loop across many foci. It involves staying agile, responsive, and open to new opportunities as the landscape changes around you. While many of us embrace the power of multitasking, fluxive leadership sets a simple tone for your mental state by classifying your numerous tasks as "orienting" for or "acting" on. In this sense, tasks are either waiting for information or action. The fluid part of this mindset is that, at any point, you can jump from orienting to acting or from acting to orienting. It's a distinct and active awareness of continuous forward motion in knowledge and activity. Details on the two phases that make up this infinite cycle are as follows:

> Orientation: Fluxive leaders are hands-on with their teams, and they dig into the details of how things work here. With such depth of knowledge, you can only identify problems and potential obstacles and look for ways to overcome them. The "lead by doing" approach builds trust and enthusiasm for teams to embrace change. They have a natural bias for "doing" that consistently leads to tangibles. They are so obsessed with knowing how the company functions and visualizing what will happen next that they rarely prove invaluable. A world of work is abundant; adaptability requires recognition and cultivation of these doers.

Orientation, as a phase, involves mapping the terrain and setting goals and tactics for getting there. Any situation where you don't have enough information to act should be considered Orientating. Some questions that come up during this phase include, but are not limited to:

> Where am I now? Hence, evaluate your assets, strengths, and the market environment to determine your current position.
> Where do I want to go? Set clear vision-centric, measurable, and path goals.
> How do I get there? Explore your area(s) of interest and develop or expand your roadmap. Like all journeys in life, the roadmap can be as simple as driving down the street or as complicated as going across the country. Set an expected course and adjust along the way.
> Do I have all the required data to act? Is there anything I can do to understand my feelings and myself better? If you need to learn more, research or consult experts to gather data.

Depending on where you are and what needs attention, a strategy reevaluation can be anything from a brief check-in to a complete one. Its purpose is to pave the way for action.

Action: The action phase isn't overly complicated; it's executing the activities you've oriented to. It's a phase where you carry out the plans and strategies established, create artifacts, act, and continuously move toward your goals. Action is where correctly oriented visions, at least until you know otherwise, become reality. Act now and review as you overcome difficulties and reach your highest peak.

In doing so, torch-passing leaders monitor how the new standard plays out, collect feedback, and fine-tune this postconflict phase. They seek ways to iterate on the premise that even a good solution can become stale as conditions change. So, they loop back on the orientation phase and start it all over again to keep that cycle of continuous improvement spinning.

Critical considerations while acting include:

- Execution of tasks and activities that need to be done.
- Observation of extended context outside the oriented scope for further awareness and additional orientation.
- Continuous evaluation of the activities as they align with the designated purpose.

Though each cycle might sound exceedingly simple, fluxive leaders realize that every element of an organization is engaged and riding countless other cycles. In the interest of growing together, they focus on those stuck or faltering and adjust their attention accordingly. Fluxive leaders, familiar with these cycles and the allocation of attention required to control them effectively, can sustain momentum in everything they influence.

Fluxive leadership is an ongoing tango between direction and activity. Leaders who master this mental dance will find ways to move forward under any circumstances and lead their organizations toward a future of innovation, adaptability, and ongoing success.

Cultivating an Innovation Culture

A self-feeding cycle, especially that of fluxive leadership, helps create an organizational culture built for change. Leaders innovate and drive change, proactively adapting by assessing, acting, standardizing, and refining. Such agility is necessary to survive the pace of change that defines our world today.

Conventional leadership models tend to disregard high-value "soft power" players, that is, those working behind the curtain, and concentrate only on what happens at the top. Fluxive leaders, as bottom-up motivators, primarily unseen and unrecognized, counterbalance, keeping the organization sharp and working alongside teams while maintaining an all-rounded momentum. "Information is power and modern information technology is spreading information more widely than ever before in history."[26]

Fluxive leaders recognize the power of information, value the unsung heroes, promote new ways of thinking, and emphasize enterprise success over compartmentalized duties. As a result, these fluid leaders step in and assist cross-functional teams, creating the collaborative and trusting atmosphere required to keep up with the spread of information on technology.

The concept of fluxive leadership, characterized by adaptability and a willingness to embrace change, is not limited to those in managerial positions. It's a powerful asset for anyone navigating the complexities of the AI era as "power is the ability to influence the behavior of others to get the outcomes one wants."[26]

Fluxive leaders embody a thoughtful and deliberate approach to judgment and decision making. One that is rooted in a clear understanding of advancing organizational values. They regularly pause and even stop to question their current position and direction, ensuring alignment with their overarching goals, critically examining the factors influencing their choices, and striving for clarity and intentionality.

With predictive analysis becoming the new order as AI takes over, human judgment and value-based decision making cannot be emphasized more now than ever. Although AI can uncover valuable insights and predictions from organizational data, the human workforce must trust or doubt them (in proper alignment and context) based on their understanding of these conclusions and considerations around potential social harm/benefit associated with implementing recommendations.

In the AI era, direction is more than knowing where you are, your past, and what the future holds for you; it's also the continuous alignment over time. It demands a clear direction and is driven by the collective efforts of those working together toward one joint mission.

An organization with leadership that can navigate this tension of autonomy and interdependence will be successful in this new world. By engaging broad and unique perspectives in a context of shared outcomes, organizations can maximize the complementary strengths between humans—who lend credibility to their extensive experience on one end—and artificial intelligence, which offers meaningful support based upon data trends on the other. The AI era is a once-in-a-career transformational opportunity for individuals and their organizations. Adopting fluxive leadership, emphasizing alignment, and leveraging human and machine intelligence provide agility to support long-term success.

Mapping Invisible Forces

The pace of organizational change required to adapt and coevolve alongside the current landscape has given rise to the need for cross-function behavior analysis. A new role, yet to be formally recognized, has started to fill this void. Emerging as transformative and vital, influence architects rise above traditional titles and hierarchies to peel the organization's layers back. These fluxive unicorns blend information analysis, artificial intelligence, behavioral science, and strategy to build the organization's influence architecture. They can recognize, interpret, and operate within an organization's intertwining frameworks. By doing so, they offer a supreme advantage in devising strategies aligning with the organization's mission, goals, and long-term ambition and using them to mold internal dynamics. They go beneath the surface of the operation, breaking down teams and departments and inspecting key staff. More than mere org chart checkers, they meticulously and painstakingly dissect the roles, responsibilities, and workflows to identify nodes of influence—channels where resources can accelerate flow through an organization.

Influence architects work daily to gain insights into how decisions are made and how change is affected within and in support of the organization by carefully mapping the currents of influence, many of which hover invisibly in and around more formal processes.

Aligning Objectives With Influence: A Strategic Imperative

The influence architect goes beyond internal analysis by connecting organizational forces with a larger framed influence map. Influence points are adjoined to their organizational purpose, performance measures, and broader strategic ambitions—the level of strategic impact, interactions, and dependencies weigh influence points. Meticulous care keeps the organization from haphazardly spending influence; instead, it is strictly concentrated on moving the most critical desires forward.

All about motion, the architects' influence doesn't stop there; they know that organizations are not dormant inanimate things but living beings who always move according to the forces of nature they exist within. Such commitment means adaptiveness, knowing that sustainability rests in continual adoption and change—when the market evolves, strategies evolve, or new leadership emerges, so must the influence map.

The Influence Architect's Journey: Analysis to Action

To effectively navigate the complexity of hidden forces, the influence architect uses a structured method consisting of:

Analyzing the organization: By continually observing and mapping the interaction process from within an organization, possibilities for manifesting influence begin to present themselves. Mapping the work and interactions helps to expose organizational vantage points where command can influence aspects such as team structures, personnel, hierarchy, or workforce spread. Knowing how your organization thinks, works, and what it believes in paints a complete picture of your influence architecture scaffolding: the vantage points, perspectives, designated activities, and overall organizational flow.

Defining activity and responsibilities: When we map the organization, it is necessary to have felt thought as deep analysis production where we will validate the roles and perspectives of each unit or individual. The main points that determine the alignment of an organization are their contributions and interactions. Further scrutiny reveals misalignments or places in which, as they harmonize, we can perform better as an organization.

Identifying critical points of interest (POIs): POIs are critical places within an organizational system—organizational structure, processes, and systems that make it relatively easier to exacerbate—that pose as leverage in steering the organization with strategic intent. These POIs suggest pathways leading to influence the decision making or behaviors of individuals rather than with overt power or coercion. Knowing these milestones guides us in positioning ourselves better in the organizational flow and driving desired results seamlessly.

Weighting influence points: Determining which influence points to pursue can be challenging and is a function of the organization's mission and objectives in the near and long term. The most influential points that match these functions form the critical paths, allowing you to focus on those efforts that provide value and help achieve your goals. Prioritizing this way also ensures that you distribute resources evenly and do the most to get what you want out of your influence.

Assessing interactions and impact: Critical touchpoints in the organizational workflow. Analyzing these provides a deep dive to determine where strategic intervention can impact the experience. These touchpoints are decision points, communications, or collaboration signpost moments where a gentle nudge or intervention can have far-reaching implications. You can also enrich the quality of routines at either an individual or team level in the workplace, eventually leading to a more productive, healthier, and happier working environment. It enhances efficiency, innovation, and overall business performance.

Enriching the corporate mission: Every influence point within and beyond the organization's boundaries must be carefully designed to resonate with a larger corporate mission /operational goal. This way, every strategic intervention causes individual actions and leads to further hopes for the organization and a unified purpose for business.

Aligning to long-term influence: By imposing your influence tactics over a long-term period in line with the strategic roadmap, you are guaranteed that your initiatives not only provide short-term tangible outcomes but also infuse and manifest their way from now into eternity, ensuring that growth and victory are sustainable. Including influence initiatives with the larger strategic vision demonstrates a unified and powerful approach to effectively move work plans forward with relevant short-term wins and sustained long-term growth for the organization.

Being a Fluxive Leader

Influence architects embrace a more fluid style of leadership to maintain strategic coherence and effective deployment. They constantly monitor internal shifts and adjust strategies to sustain continued investment in the organization's changing needs. A fluxive mindset helps them manage complexities while anticipating and steering through issues in advance to ensure that the organization is heading in the right direction.

Careful inquiry and a holistic foundation lay the course for functional influence mapping, leading to our ability to operationalize evolutionary organizational change over time. In doing so, leaders enabled through the change agents can determine whether they will continue to experience proactively changing plans or internal dynamics to shape future outcomes for more sustained growth and success.

Dealing with invisible forces can seem like a hopeless effort requiring otherworldly capabilities. Thankfully, supporting an organization is much more about knowing where to look and using the correct lenses. Both require a mental shift, as there are no vision goggles capable of tracking these items, at least not yet. Fluxive leadership provides a framework to manage hidden forces in the turbulent and competitive market to support expanding minds and provide a solid foundation. It is not only a way for executives to work—but every team member can also apply a fluxive attitude, finding comfort in change and taking advantage of any opportunities for improvement.

Traditional approaches have typically relied on static baselines, quickly becoming outdated with change. The fluxive model, however, teaches the mental capacity to comprehend a moving baseline that attracts inescapable adjustments to objectives and circumstances. It is a malleable touchstone—the equivalent of making a check-in point that marks where you currently are about your first objectives and leaves room for things not going according to plan in such a way that unlocks the full potential of continuous improvement, where your organization is built to absorb and capitalize on change.

The Fluxive Mindset: Balance in the Cycle of Thinking and Acting

In the same way that yin and yang in ancient Chinese philosophy represent a dualistic, interdependent life cycle, the fluxive mindset loops us back into performing two essential human functions: orienting ourselves and making choices. It is an elegant and beautiful acknowledgment that we can contemplate what to do next at any given moment or enact the plan of waking up to life.

It is a mindset that accepts the ebb and flow of the world around us. We are constantly in flux between reflection and action. Often, we must stop, collect data, and evaluate the circumstances before taking steps. Sometimes, we must act boldly and take our best guess. During both observation and reflection, we still are subconsciously doing the other.

Life may feel less heavy when we accept that everything is a cycle and let go of the idea that we must control everything. We will also begin to accept that there will always be unknowns and uncertainty, which is alright. The fluxive mindset helps on multiple levels:

Reduces anxiety and stress: Acknowledging the normal split-bound-edness of organizational life, fluxive leadership sings in discreet harmony to the inherent ebbs and flows of systemic thought and performance. By recognizing the inevitability of change and embracing it as a part of the process, anxiety, and stress are lowered by increasing adaptability and resilience. So, instead of expending effort and energy in pushing against change or clinging to a fixed point, the fluxive leader recognizes that all things are in motion and ready their team for the changing tides that will come with time.

Skyrocket adaptability: As a dynamic approach, fluxive leadership is a celebrant of change, processing new experiences as adaptive resiliency and embodying evolution; a fluxive mentality establishes a community within constant transition. A fluid understanding, which recognizes the inevitability of evolving conditions, promotes an attitude of adaptiveness—or readiness to respond to new challenges. The mindset helps to become present, choosing intentionally in thought and action so that individuals and teams can make more thoughtful choices and get favorable results despite uncertainty. Fluxive leadership increases the ability of an organization to be adaptable and resilient in a constantly changing environment, catapulting them far ahead of any other leader who does not promote these qualities.

Creates a mentality of options: Fluxive leadership fosters a mind-set of options by emphasizing the power of choice. This motivates people to actively seek out and embrace experiences and outcomes rather than passively accepting them. By recognizing the importance of choice and empowering individuals, fluxive leadership creates an active and engaged workforce with a sense of control over their actions and contributions to the organization's success.

A fluxive mindset applies not only to the professional field but also to personal development. It can further help individuals on a personal level through:

Enhanced decision making: We can never have perfect foresight, but a fluxive attitude helps us stop and think before we respond to situations. As we create space between stimulus and response, we have time to collect information, consider alternative perspectives, and decide more from our power.

Improved resilience: A fluxive mindset enables individuals to remain flexible and resilient, allowing them to roll with the punches of any sudden challenge or speed bump. Instead of walling up in front of change or getting upset, we move diagonally and get faster at identifying solutions and paths we did not see before.

Develop a growth mindset: A fluxive mindset encourages approach challenges to learn and grow. This forces people to step out of their comfort zones and confront any action, good or bad, with open curiosity to learn as much from each action (and success) as possible.

Personal well-being: A mindset that promotes mindfulness and acceptance of change in one's life helps one deal with stress better and brings one more inner peace. Regulating oneself to be present and react to the natural changes of life leads to greater emotional resilience, both professionally and personally.

At its core, the fluxive mindset is a resilient structure for navigating personal and professional life with ease and gentle strength. It reminds us that we can always think or act and know when thinking should be the choice.

Fluxivity as a Dynamic Approach to Orientation and Action

Embarking on any transformative journey requires a clear understanding of your starting point. The "orienting" phase of the fluxive mindset centers on gaining a comprehensive grasp of your current state:

Understand where you are: A thorough audit of your existing information, process flow, and KPIs is essential. This evaluation will illuminate your strengths and weaknesses, revealing areas where AI can be readily integrated and those that may require further preparation.

Gather quantitative and qualitative insights: Go beyond mere numbers. Combine quantitative data (sales figures, website traffic) with qualitative insights (customer feedback, employee observations). This holistic approach provides a multifaceted understanding of your current landscape.

Set evidence-based objectives: Collaborate with leadership to define measurable goals that AI integration will support. This focused approach ensures that your efforts are directed toward achieving tangible and impactful outcomes.

With a solid understanding of your current state and clearly defined objectives, it's time to take action. The "acting" phase of the fluxive mindset involves moving forward with purpose while remaining adaptable to new information and challenges:

Embrace flexibility: Sometimes, the path ahead is clear, and progress is a matter of straightforward execution. However, at other times, you should take exploratory steps to gather more information and reorient yourself along the way.

Iterate and learn: Be bold, experiment, and adjust your approach as needed. View setbacks as learning opportunities and use them to refine your strategies.

Maintain momentum: Keep moving forward, even when uncertain. The fluxive mindset encourages a bias toward action tempered by a willingness to course-correct as necessary, even if that action is further observation.

The fluxive mindset, emphasizing orientation and action, provides a robust framework for navigating the complexities of the AI era. It encourages organizations to be strategic and adaptable, empowering them to embrace change, seize opportunities, and achieve their goals in an ever-evolving landscape.

Organizational Fluxivity: Foundations for Concepts to Actions

Unleash the Organization's Collective Potential and Empower Decentralized Decision Making!

Knowing how to navigate leadership in a brave new world is empowering. Whether you're leading yourself, a team, or an entire organization, embracing change and flexing your style isn't just important; it's liberating. In a world of rapid change, traditional leadership with static metrics in isolation curtails an organization's potential capabilities. For authentic leadership to emerge, adaptability and flexibility must embody this principle; dependence on KPIs can mislead.

While metrics are focused, the environment around them can change. Consider a retail store that reduces its hours due to a staffing shortage.

Do old sales targets based on longer hours apply?
Would it be right to take only the sales from our new open hours?

Direct inquiries remind us how ignoring changes in your audiences' behavior due to your organization's changing expectations can be highly damaging. Changing the context changes people's actions because you break existing patterns that hold up your organization. Simple shifts could result in confusion, pushback, and even resentment for the lack of support for a mutually supportive pattern the audience has built with your organization. It is essential to recognize these modifications in behavior and deal with them accordingly instead. Discuss the rationale of changes, coach the team and the audience during the transition, and dialogue with everyone so expectations are clear and accepted. You help ease the crossover and keep your followers engaged and trusting. What else can we learn from this?

For one, the metrics don't make behavior.
For another, sometimes we don't have evidence for what's next.

As insight-driven leaders emerge as trend-spotters, they must also become comfortable with the paradox of surprise-causing uncertainty.

Collecting the whole gamut of data and going beyond traditional metrics may not give you any relative insights, let alone accurate ones, for what's next. The power of unfiltered employee feedback, true audience sentiment, and direct process observation are external guidelines that give your knowledge a more nuanced explanation of hidden side effects and unspoken opportunities that the sheer numbers cannot provide.

Furthermore, organizational knowledge leaders, as individuals or managers, can gain a glimpse of unknown behaviors by creating cultures of experimentation within safe boundaries. Through this, teams may innovate, sparking alignment that allows the organization to become meticulously influential in the future. It also encompasses reacting to change and actively leading into a future shaped through innovation. Combined with a fluxive mindset, the organization builds the capacity to make the most of the volatility from which change may come again.

Deep within the fallacy of the status quo, organizations without a fluxive mindset are bladed leaders, lacking teams that experiment, iterate, and innovate in this constantly evolving world. A mental shift toward fluxivity is hopeful in this changing terrain as organizations begin to accept its contours and become increasingly optimistic, ready to embrace whatever challenges or opportunities arise. A necessary shift, it fosters a harmonious coexistence of action and reaction, cultivating an environment of perpetual directly aligned innovation with the organization's vision, and acts as a guiding North Star. A collaborative and shared direction fosters team collaboration combined with clear and consistent communication, translating this vision into a unified path forward.

Resilience is no longer a luxury but a necessity for organizations. Strategies, metrics, and the overarching vision must be flexible and adaptable, ready to evolve in response to new challenges and opportunities. Leaders now face the delicate task of inspiring and motivating their teams while acknowledging the inherent uncertainty of the future. The traditional approach of delivering grand, unwavering visions may no longer be practical. Today's leaders must exercise caution and transparency, acknowledging that tomorrow's reality may necessitate adjustments to today's inspiring words. A fluxive approach helps to maintain trust and credibility, preventing teams from feeling disillusioned or misled when circumstances require a shift in direction as the shifts become part of the organization's fluxivity.

Leaders must communicate the destination and be willing to adjust the course as required, empower teams to embrace change, foster a sense of shared ownership, and build resilience in uncertainty. It's about inspiring through an ever-evolving vision and a dynamic, continuous learning, adaptation, and growth process. One that embodies a fluid foundation to transform the organization into a living, breathing entity that adapts and responds to change. Open communication ensures human teams and AI systems are aligned, preparing for the coming Machineforce Era, minimizing fears of job displacement, and empowering individuals to embrace AI's vast potential.

The Holy Trinity of Information Management: A Foundation for the AI-Driven Future

Organizations require powerful information management strategies in a world of data deluge to do well. "The Holy Trinity," as I like to call it, provides an all-encompassing framework for organizational information management and boils down to three core behaviors—standardization, understanding, and interaction. It is a trifecta of operations that helps when it comes to making data-driven decisions. It promotes awareness and practices to sustain a fluxive mindset, thereby enabling the conception of organizations with technology woven into their behavior, especially when intelligent machines converge with human workforces. Classification and expectation for technical environments to guide organizational information management are elucidated in the following three areas.

The Left Pillar

Standardization and Measurement

Your Organizational Bedrock of Alignment and Integrity.   Standardization's left pillar of this trinity emphasizes establishing consistent and reliable data collection, storage, analysis, and measurement processes.

Unsurprisingly, this involves implementing clear standards and protocols to ensure data integrity and comparability across the organization. In other words, this is how the organization tracks and measures its behavior. Transactional systems like enterprise resource planning and customer relationship management platforms play a vital role in capturing and managing structured data in a standardized manner. Certified reporting from these and business intelligence systems should also be included to support measurements. From the left pillar's perspective, models typically correspond to the expanded MRM category of Alignment AI.

The Center Pillar

Orientation

Your Flexible Investigation and Understanding Sandbox. The center pillar, orientation, focuses on deeply understanding stakeholders' needs, preferences, and readiness for change. This necessitates active listening and engagement through various channels, such as surveys, interviews, focus groups, and data analysis. Flexible and investigatory environments like data lakes, on-demand data science platforms, and business intelligence systems facilitate data exploration and analysis, generating insights into stakeholder behaviors and preferences. The left pillar can then codify insights into organizational standards, while the right pillar can include supporting interactive modules. By actively demonstrating empathy and fostering open communication, organizations can build trust with stakeholders and anticipate their evolving needs, ensuring their strategies and offerings remain relevant in a dynamic market. From the center pillar's perspective, models typically correspond to the expanded MRM category of investigative AI.

The Right Pillar

Interaction

Your AI-Powered Situational Awareness System. The right pillar, interaction, is your interactive facade for monitoring, acting, and adapting in real time. Organizations must establish systematic processes for real-time data collection and analysis, enabling them to identify trends, anticipate risks, and seize opportunities. Predictive analytics further empowers them to forecast market shifts and adjust strategies, ensuring long-term growth and sustainability. Real-time streaming platforms, alerting systems, and production AI models enable continuous monitoring and analysis of data streams, allowing for timely decision making and proactive responses to changing conditions. From the right pillar's perspective, models typically correspond to the expanded MRM category of influential AI.

Bridging Technology and Organizational Behavior

The Holy Trinity framework represents a crucial blueprint for organizations to organize technology to harness AI responsibly and effectively in the workplace. Aligning your technology to three building blocks —standardization, understanding, and engagement—sets the stage for data-driven decision making, drives stakeholder participation around a common language resonating with a shared context, and builds a culture of partnership.

Standardization is responsible for keeping the data clean and comparable to the organization, making it easier for the team to communicate and analyze. Understanding dives further into stakeholder requirements and interprets these informed required increases in data analytics understanding to anticipate and be versatile at need. The interaction pillar, meanwhile, enables organizations to monitor in real time how their network of organizational interactions engages and takes the actions needed to capitalize on opportunities, mitigate risk, or successfully adapt to changing trends.

The Holy Trinity framework aims to orient organizations on the right path for implementing responsible AI, maximizing the benefits of its due diligence within ethical boundaries. Such a holistic view enables organizations to make more competent decisions and lays the groundwork for long-term alignment in a machineforce-centric future.

Keys to Informed Adaptation

Adaptation is not just reactive—it's also a decision, a fluxive choice, to change in response to changing circumstances. Fluxive leadership's semifocus redirects our understanding of where we are now and where we want to be. This self-awareness lets us navigate intricacies and ambiguities, providing a vision of where to set our sights and scorecards to measure results as the world reconfigures. This encourages proactive change instead of reactive deterioration. We gain a strategic height simply by welcoming change and establishing resilience nodes in us for accelerated growth. Adapting to a place of adaptability helps us survive and, even more importantly, thrive in an ever-changing world. Here are the keys to informed adaptation:

Position and direction: Establishing a position is not simply about pinpointing your current location on a map or within an industry. It goes beyond a simple pin in a map—it's about establishing a comprehensive and fluid baseline that encompasses your contextual perspective, setting the stage for future movement and growth. To establish positioning:

Defining your interest: Identify your organization's specific area or aspect you want to explore, improve, or transform. This could be a process, department, product, or strategic objective.

Conducting a thorough evaluation: Take the time to analyze and document your current practices, resources, capabilities, and any existing benchmarks or performance indicators. Evaluation will reveal your strengths and weaknesses and highlight opportunities for potential improvement, providing a clear picture of your starting point.

Quantify and frame qualitative observations: Break down and provide context to turn qualitative insights into measurements that can be acted upon, allowing progress to be tracked results reviewed, and trends observed. It is necessary to compare framing (how the data were collected, under what circumstances, and context) between changes to proximate the contextual change and data quantifications. Turning your observations into measures

allows you to monitor, analyze, and take appropriate actions
effectively, thus unlocking data-driven decisions.

Establishing a system for future comparisons: Develop a systematic
approach to capturing and documenting your evaluation methods
to ensure consistency in future assessments. This will enable
performance comparisons and measurement of the impact of any
changes or interventions.

Defining the scope of activities and focus gives teams a launch-
ing point for improvements. An established foundation becomes a
measuring rod to show progress; otherwise, it clarifies what needs
improvement, which helps direct decision making and focus on patterns
with solid motivators. If your well-articulated stance is developed wisely,
even the best-positioned image in a frame of exquisite bone or exotic
wood would still be of little worth to you without that compass. No
matter how sophisticated or complex, a map shows just the territory.
In life, the compass works as a guide: It tells us which way to go with
nuanced precision throughout its entire direction.

Similarly, knowing where you are now is critical regarding strategy,
whether organizational or personal development, but it's the first step.
It would be best to have a compass—an overview, structured approach,
or behavioral principles to keep advancing toward your goals. All this
sounds good, but without that sense of direction, your well-defined
position becomes static, which doesn't satisfy its reason for being. It's a
pretty picture with no purpose!

We can only get to where we want to be by figuring out who we are
and deciding which way our compass points. This combination forms
a valuable compass that will keep us on track with our challenges and
opportunities and point us to success. Principles that apply universally:

Data-driven decision making: Descriptive details and historical data
offer insights into model placement, while diagnostics inform
machine learning trajectories, enabling continuous improvement
through informed decisions.

Proactive security: Shift from prediction to protection. Align safeguards with behavioral patterns to reduce risk and effectively navigate ambiguity.

Strategic clarity: Maintain a macro-viewpoint to embed contextual understanding across a broader spectrum. This prevents getting lost in details and ensures strategic objectivity.

The more turbulent and uncertain the environment, the better you need to grip your positions and course. Extended situational awareness becomes your guiding light on worsening days of unexpected challenges or new behaviors, reminding you to stay fluxive, reorient, and make active decisions consciously. Recognizing and being mindful of issues and being willing to experience empathy can convert these challenges into opportunities. Prioritizing evidence-based decisions, open dialogue, and proactive pivots empower us to move with purpose through global nuances. Routine assessment, combined with a meta-view of the space where our ambitions lie, allows us to evolve forward: adapting and learning along this process forever.

Boundaries

Defining good boundaries that support adaptation at the organizational level requires a researcher's curiosity to discover hidden trends, the sensibility of a behavioral scientist for human reactions, and an in-depth understanding of how your organization works. But the good news is— that this treasure trove of experience and insights can be boiled down to a more efficient exercise in identifying where maintaining distinctions with your current roles or future path is necessary. The following are some excellent rules for setting boundaries:

Supportive, not restrictive: For boundaries to be effective, they must provide direction, follow an enabling rather than restricting mindset, and actively align with the target user without creating conflicts. By fostering a safe and structured environment, boundaries create the conditions for innovation to grow.

Proactive, not reactive: The best boundaries are the ones you set before they are urgently needed. This allows for planning rather than reactionary behavior. However, it can be hard to be proactive when the future is unknown or we're developing an entirely new process. In this context, AI can help build scenarios showing what to look for.

Balanced, not one-sided: When working correctly, your goals are meant to slip into the background, lightly tucked within your workflow so you forget you're hungry and feel in control without self-restriction.

Seamless, not intrusive: Ideally, boundaries should operate in the background, seamlessly integrated into the workflow, so that individuals feel empowered, not restricted. They should facilitate operations without imposing additional friction or barriers and so on.

Setting effective boundaries is essential to facilitate adaptiveness in an organization. It ensures AI is auxiliary in setting up preventive, merged, and preintegrated bounds within workflows. There are several significant barriers to where AI can become an ally:

Scenario planning: AI can create scenarios to identify potential boundary gaps which challenge may be exception or excused for proactive planning (not reactive action).

Tailored boundaries: AI could be responsible for creating work boundaries that support rather than limit by learning individual needs and preferences.

Real-time monitoring: AI could monitor activities and interactions, picking up red flags for boundary violations while gently reminding or nudging all participants to stay the course. AI can take this information further by automatically identifying how an individual and team are performing, allowing for identifying patterns/trends that could be used when moving boundaries.

Conflict resolution: AI can help oversee health communication and mediation when boundary conflict arises, supporting early amicable resolutions.

Organizations can transform into an environment where boundaries drive innovation, empower people, and facilitate operational efficiencies using AI. Practical boundary setting represents a "motionless means of interacting"—a subtle yet powerful influence that shapes behavior without overt action. It's essential to recognize that even boundaries can appear to create movement within a dynamic environment, much like a seemingly static object in a game of motion—a condition where boundaries are executed, appearing invisible but supporting alignment so as not to hinder progress. Fostering a fertile environment empowers the organization, teams, and individuals to innovate and achieve optimal alignment, which happens symbiotically within clear, supportive boundaries that promote freedom and fluxivity.

Dynamic Adaptation

It's frequently said that the only constant is change, and in a world of unyielding velocity, organizations that refuse to adapt will lose. To embrace adaptability is to accept that change will happen, and for an organization to survive, it must develop a culture of innovation and evolution. Adaptability plays a vital role in survival and has become the ultimate need, especially with ongoing advancements in technology and AI. Historically, adaptability has centered around significant product offerings, services, or changes in business operations. Business intelligence platforms run descriptive and diagnostic analytics to show current standing, past performance, and opportunities for improvement. These elements of insight help address issues, respond to emerging trends, and navigate challenges.

Adaptability in the age of AI presents us with an iterative vision, with insights from AI only as rails and guideposts for cruising through uncharted territories. Insight provides both predictive and prescriptive capabilities, offering a path of best fit or at least warning skirts (much like the bumpers you put up in bowling lanes). For instance, audience sentiment and feedback on social media are valuable data that AI systems can analyze to identify specific audience groups and tailor influential messages to them. A targeted approach can shift overall sentiment from negative to positive.

Integrating an AI-powered "machineforce" across the company as workforce partners can enable employees to adapt quickly to change and respond effectively to dynamic environments. Intelligent machineforces can further aid this process by providing comprehensive contextual evidence, boundaries, and guidance. The additional flexibility empowers them to make more informed, strategic decisions with greater participation and a long-term perspective.

With machine learning, AI systems use historical data to predict outcomes consistent with previously observed behavior to increase efficiency and yield positive results. But we frequently misinterpret predictions as inflexible roadmaps, indexes capable of dishing up lottery numbers or scorecards for athletic events. Such a view completely ignores the true power of AI to make one adaptable, which should give its users confidence. AI predictions are not immutable; they are informed constraints!

In the same way, riverbed channels flow, and filters map out what is likely, given our current understanding. Riverbeds can erode, and filters are not forever; they change with new inputs and dynamics. Remember early GPS navigation? When we get initial directions to our destination from our current location, those original instructions need to tell us where accidents on the road are or if a particular street will be closed that evening. Thankfully, nowadays, GPS systems include traffic and alternate routes around long backups. In the same way, dynamic environments such as warehouses or supply chains almost certainly require daily, if not real time, updates to AI predictions for any relevance.

With time dependencies come drawbacks, such as a particular set of forecasts focusing on a specific point in time and the data available to represent it. However, these results may be helpful as guideposts for actions (e.g., when restocking inventory or fulfilling orders). Imagine looking at a weather forecast: it does not locate every single raindrop, but you decide to take an umbrella. In the same way, AI's efforts fall short of predicting individual customer responses; they are too hyper-focused, but rather global trends that help marketing tactics and anticipate business changes.

Re-envisioning forecasts as guardrails that AI helps inform opens the power and richness of responsive systems powered by humans to their fullest potential. It is now an instrument of coping with ambiguity, not obliterating it, and embracing supple adaptation rooted in emergent pathways rather than deterministic ones. Use data-driven insights as guardrails of directional support to better navigate the world around us, changing faster than we can get ahead of it—instead of operating under scenario-based planning so you are not trying to cancel and control everything. It may sound like an excellent concept of an adaptable organization. However, turning adaptability into a reality that can handle uncertainty, take a toll, and allow for different outcomes requires actual work. It is a crucial and refreshing focus for the organization.

Fluxive team members and leaders welcome change and constantly seek opportunities to evolve. "To encourage dissenting views, some managers explicitly give one person the job of constantly voicing an opposing perspective. It encourages people with that particular perspective to speak up and other alternative viewpoints."[28] With extended perspectives, the team can identify desired resources, make changes on a trial basis, and study the effects closely. Improved efficiency, audience satisfaction, and profitability would be tangible value. The appropriate enhancement is then identified and standardized across the company to become part of its general operating procedure.

Embodying the fluxive cycle promotes a learning culture, encourages experimentation, and keeps adaptation not as an event but flowing continually. Adopting this maxim and approach, organizations can skillfully advance uncertainty for assured resistance amidst changes to the industry or landscape. The feedback loops all organizations desire to move from sidebar check-ins and surveys to a normal part of the cycle at all levels. It should remind the team of longer-term promises and obligations, another reason to jump on with relentless changes. While simple in representation and steps, fluxive leadership provides a systematic method for developing adaptability and creativity in your organization.

Choreography and Force Blueprints

Every plan you make is stymied; the workplace—or at least where it happens—is also a maze, exhausting even for professed navigators eager to transform from fixed structures into sleek and sentient people machines. As such, we need to develop a much greater understanding of how organizational workflows operate—in theory and beyond what is described on paper. With workforces increasingly working locally and beyond the traditional command-and-control structures, contextual awareness is only set to become more critical.

Much of this complexity trap is part and parcel of concluding that many current organizations face challenges because they deal with world linearity in complex environments. Keep in mind that figuring things out can be challenging. We often need more resources, tools, or motivation to chase a solution. Appropriate: It looks at bottlenecks, repaired communication gaps, and cut slack. Embrace a tactical orientation to transformation! It is not enough to have a good attitude when navigating complex organizations; one must be deliberate and recognize the subtleties of an organization and help focus efforts toward transformational change. Competent, strategic, and with clear goals, innovation occurs in all company areas by thinking strategically. Prepare for the marathon, not the sprint.

Organizations must pace themselves and realize that there are hills ahead, just as marathoners do. Focusing solely on the short-term and fast returns means overwork, burnout, and much slower progress in the long run. With a fluxive mindset, strive to create an equilibrium between benefit and natural order. Slowing down and being mindful is critical for guiding you toward your vision and sustainable organizational growth.

Influential Blueprints: The Art of Orchestration

Creating blueprints for human–machine collaboration is akin to choreographing a complex dance, where every movement, interaction, and transition is meticulously planned and executed. Like a symphony, the goal is a harmonious blend of individual contributions, resulting

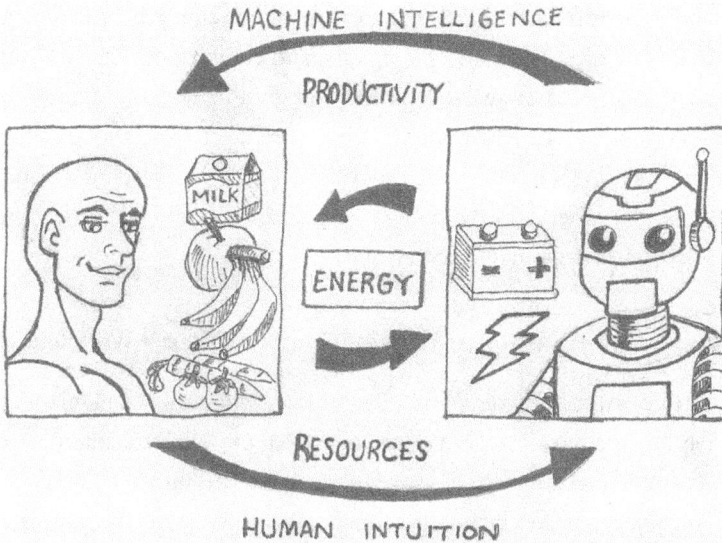

Figure 5.2 The symbiotic circuit: A visual metaphor for human–AI collaboration

in a unified and impactful outcome. While the symphony metaphor captures the essence of collaborative synergy, it might imply a level of conscious coordination between humans and machines that is only sometimes present. The interaction between humans and AI is often more subtle and nuanced. Imagine yourself as an audience member at a symphony. You witness the seamless interplay of instruments, each contributing a unique melody to the composition. You're unaware of the individual musicians' thought processes or the sheet music they follow, but you experience a harmonious result. The influence architects' perspective aims to achieve human–machine collaboration. In this seamless interplay, the individual actions of humans and AI blend effortlessly to create a unified and impactful outcome (Figure 5.2).

The influence architect, much like a conductor, doesn't microman-age every action. Instead, they set the overall direction, establish the structure, and ensure that each element—human and machine—contributes effectively to the collective goal. They create the conditions for organic collaboration, fostering an environment where humans and machines work together intuitively and efficiently, requiring a deep understanding of human behavior and intelligent machine capability.

It's about identifying and leveraging each's unique strengths, recognizing that humans excel at creativity, empathy, and complex decision making, while AI excels at data analysis, pattern recognition, and automation. By orchestrating this interplay, the influence architect fosters an environment where collaboration and innovation flourish. It's about creating a symphony where the combined output of humans and machines surpasses what either could achieve alone.

Crafting Force Blueprints: Your Influence Architect's Workflow

The AI era, and next, the Machineforce Era, will require organizations to rely on a strategic roadmap to maneuver the intricate interplay of humans and machines. Please meet the influence architect, who can design blueprints for blending human capabilities with AI powers in harmony toward complementary objectives. Let's compose a symphony where each player (human or machine) brings their best and creates an impactful performance together.

Influence Architecture Workflow

1. Capture the As-Is State
   The first step is to understand your work operations. Map out every process, identify each step, and capture responsible parties. Ensure that the inputs, outputs, and decision points are identified. After itemization and a team review, this extensive overview is your map for adjusting organizational flows with AI.
2. Identify AI-Enablement Points
   Once you have documented your existing processes, figure out where it makes the most sense to strategically incorporate AI-driven tools that make tasks more efficient or automated. Find tasks that are often repeated and take much longer to manually; data analysis and pattern recognition algorithms where AI insights can guide human decision making.
3. Singling Out Tasks
   Allocate different tasks to humans and AI. Define the functions and responsibilities to be performed, along with inputs from

which AI will work on outputs it would produce, as well as decision rights—where it will act. Ports of CallThis is essential to avoid ambiguity or role duplication.

4. Human–AI Interaction

   Consider how humans will and should interact with AI. Think about how users will input into the AI, process and apply outputs produced by AIs, and work alongside an AI to decide. The aim was to create a user-friendly and optimal experience.

5. Define Triggers and Events

   Discover the events or triggers that drive AI responses, interventions, and influence. For example, in a time-based manner, for example, generating a report at the end of each month, or data-driven, that is, an alert should be sent out when specific diagnostics move beyond thresholds and change compared to the previous period.

6. Feedback Loops

   Create a mechanism that provides feedback on how humans and AI perform conceptually. This will enable continuing education and development of AI algorithms, enabling the system to maintain effectiveness while addressing evolving needs.

7. Embrace Evolution, Refactor, and Repeat

   The blueprints are anything but static and should continually evolve as your organization grows along with AI capabilities. Iterate and update your blueprints based on regular feedback, data analysis, and business constraints.

The ability of AI to automate redundant tasks thus provides competitive leverage through workforce and machineforce blueprints as it empowers more human resources to think and act strategically. Moreover, AI's high data processing capability enables companies to make more informed decisions based on hitting goals. The speed of AI also allows organizations to react rapidly to market changes and customer demands. By getting AI assistance, employee engagement is undoubtedly better as they can focus more on things that value their creativity and problem-solving ability. While building and executing these playbooks is an ongoing process, it will enable a company to achieve AI's full potential and establish the necessary framework to encourage meaningful human technology collaboration that allows maximum productivity, creativity, and, ultimately, success.

Thriving Through Change: A "Finalizing" Mentality

The most successful species on Earth are only sometimes the most powerful or the swiftest. Instead, they're the ones that demonstrate adaptability and flexibility. There's a solid argument to be made that kindness and cooperation also play a significant role in survival.[27] Organizations should adopt this evolutionary mindset, recognizing that past achievements don't guarantee future success. Rigidity can lead to stagnation in a world where change is the only constant. Clinging to outdated strategies is like trying to maintain a castle built on sand—eventually, the tide of progress will wash it away. True resilience is fluid, not a constant condition, and is not a problem in the minds of fluxive leaders, as they know those who fear change will never be able to handle it. It requires a career-long commitment to learning, fostering experimentation, and developing agile processes that can adapt to unexpected obstacles. But it's not just about the processes; it's about the people. Leaders have a crucial role in exuding trust, belonging, and purpose—the core elements of what their teams need to engage with this evolution. As a leader, you can shape your organization's future.

Change is disruptive, and knowing where you are headed will always be a rallying point in any transformation journey. Recognizing changes in the landscape caused by external events provides opportunities to adjust and meet the new normal. Change, however, is not only necessary; enlightenment and growth are a direct offshoot of change. Change is not just a part of the journey; it is the journey. Embrace it, and you'll find yourself on the path to growth and success.

The Power of Finalizing

Enter the notion of "finalizing": not an outcome to achieve but a process within fluxive leadership. It is centered on your perspective to notice the facts and decide what you do with them. It is an opportunity to reset and evolve, letting go of the preconceptions we held in our previous role but moving forward with a more explicit purpose.

SportClips, the sports-themed barber shop, turned a potential crisis during the pandemic into a feel-good story. Embracing safety measures, they didn't just comply with mask mandates; they went beyond by turning masks into a stylish brand statement. SportClips used sports-themed face masks, turning a necessary precaution into a further environmental enrichment. It wasn't just about following the rules but about exceeding expectations and staying true to their brand identity. It demonstrated that organizations could prioritize safety and delight, creating a positive experience that fosters loyalty even during challenging times.

In a nutshell, the beauty of this straightforward and very syntactic narrative lies in enabling you to adapt to managing change and for it to be your strength. They inevitably become your external drivers of momentum, and by deliberately using them against the environment, you overcome these forces, abandoning them with sustainable strength and innovation.

Life is best traversed like a naval battle, constantly adjusting to changes in tides and altering your course. This proactive level of consciousness creates a solidity and capacity to listen that provides options for choice. Take time to reflect on asking if your judgment is authentic, and also make sure that what you're doing still makes sense in the context of the changing reality surrounding you. Accept change and have an organizational mindset that embraces flexibility over becoming/remaining very rigid, as you get bogged down in the past. High-level individuals and organizations are constantly changing/evolving to meet the present and prepare for what is coming down the line. By being proactive, you gain confidence in your ability to handle uncertainty and set yourself up to act on opportunities as they come.

Alignment may also be the best single-word theme for this series. In this fluid environment, adaptability isn't just about survival—it's how you thrive. It entails embracing a flexible mindset and adopting the practices that allow your business to thrive amidst so much uncertainty, not just survive but emerge from it more robustly.

The path isn't easy; the struggles bring out our best and worst, but they pave the way for a future of perpetuation and success by accepting evolution, promoting agility where needed, and continuously learning to do things just that little bit better.

CHAPTER 6

The Machineforce Ahead

Empowerment through alignment: individuals, machines, environments.

Recognized as a learning period for good measurement, the AI era will mold decision making at all levels. Everyone will be empowered with statistical insights to make informed decisions, carving out a future where AI operates as an invisible appendage to life itself. Woven into our very tapestry, AI will be capable of tasks once reserved for human minds. Furthermore, individuals and organizations can embrace the *realm of maybe* with new comfort and confidence. It is, and will continue to be, a paradigm shift of tremendous magnitude for AI to be so profoundly integrated!

Well beyond automation, AI's power will come to support inherent human characteristics like instinct and intuition. Together, situational awareness can be dialed in, plotting courses of action with more enthusiasm and certainty. Courses leading toward success that are the fastest and most protected from doubt, waste, and unnecessary effort.

Beyond the obvious applications for the organization lie more profound possibilities for the future. Organizations will establish contextually rich information-backed cores upon which AI can base decisions and actions, slicing through the intricacies of modern times with previously unthinkable clarity and direction. A point where our journey will usher in the Machineforce Era—a future where machines are no longer tools but participate as intelligent and independent partners. Together with humans, they will operate to solve the world's most challenging problems and even merge, so organic humans are hardly distinguishable from logical adaptations. AI will also become a driving force, aligning the human race with the natural world, optimizing resource management, and initiating sustainable solutions. The Machineforce Era will recast the global job spectrum, establishing a new "thin wide line" between engineers of intelligent machines and leaders of influence.

Transitioning from the AI era to the Machineforce Era will progress only as fast as organizations come to terms with relinquishing control to intelligent machines and building the organization and societal foundations to support them. This is a critical reminder that with great power comes great responsibility. Ethical and responsible use should be anticipated, as well as extensive concerns regarding interactions, influence, functional displacement, bias, and privacy, to name a few. Organizations must educate and reskill the workforce to equip themselves and their workforce with the skills to succeed in an AI-enhance future.

In the same way, data are now valued on organizational balance sheets, so will future investments in the organizational machineforce. With the combined power of human creativity and artificial intelligence, a long history of human achievement will seem like progress at a snail's pace compared to the years ahead. That said, moving forward, our biggest disappointment ahead is not all that we've achieved but the pace at which we've achieved it. Now is the time to craft foundations for a symbiotic machineforce, setting well apart from a long past and positioning for exponential advancement.

Change as Tomorrow's Craft: Nurturing Collective Growth

The vision of an "artificially intelligent" organization is nothing short of awe-inspiring. Converting from fantasy to fact requires traversing a minefield of obstacles that test even the most dedicated enthusiasts. While tales of success present stories with many ups and downs, the human challenges behind change lead to discomfort, natural hesitancy, and resistance inside an organization, underscoring the vital need for the perpetual influence of people, redevelopment of processes, and reliance on machines to achieve harmony. It's time for all team members to become digital artists! Data are the paint, and the organization awaits as much artful insight as possible.

When stitched together, like paintings across multiple canvases, diverse perspectives catalyze innovation. By nurturing collective intelligence and embracing all perspectives, organizations will thrive not despite change but because of it. Organizations can break resistance through a culture of continuous improvement and successfully negotiate the digital transformation maze. It is not an easy journey, but the benefits of improved organizational intelligence, adaptability, and resilience are priceless. To make this journey successful, organizations can focus on and reinforce the following:

Experimenting: Develop an experimental culture where employees can explore and experiment with technologies and approaches in a safe environment to learn new things without fearing change. Build a culture that experiments, understands, and expects deeper insights.

Reinventing instead of replacing: Provide robust enablement and training; lead by example with adoption! Provide them with continuous support and additional resources to help them deal with any setbacks or problems they may have.

Delivering vision: There's always a path forward, and leaders must emphasize the organization's vision and how these new tools and technologies help achieve it. When individuals understand the "why" behind a change, they are more likely to embrace it and contribute to its success.

Appreciating and rewarding: Recognize and reward those who embrace change, follow processes, achieve results, or even fail—yes, the people who fail—in support of the organization. It's okay to fail. Human evolution is and has always been guided by failures. Embracing recognition of success and failure cements measurable engagement and activates a reinforcement cycle to evolve and move forward. Recognition of failures also provides a unique stance that even in situations that do not move things forward, the effort and quality of work are still evaluated.

Nurturing the Intelligent Organization

The future of work is plausible and should be considered a focus on artificial intelligence. The future of work belongs to "intelligent organizations," where humans and AI form a symbiotic partnership, engaging in a continuous cycle of learning and improvement. As an intelligent ecosystem of the future, humans leverage creativity, empathy, and strategic thinking to guide AI's development, ensuring its alignment with goals and values. Conversely, AI empowers humans with augmented capabilities, enhancing our decision making, automating routine tasks, and unlocking new possibilities. As a formidable team, together, continuously refining and enhancing abilities, the virtuous cycle drives innovation, productivity, and the creation of a workplace that is both fulfilling and transformative.

The result? The ability to get things done by whoever or whatever creates incredible innovation and problem-solving. To support alignment, organizations must build comprehensive knowledge systems that go well beyond data repositories and hold more profound knowledge and historical context. *Behaviors, not numbers, measure progress.*

Information curation and proper distribution is a precious activity. Collect all the data you want and organize, catalog, and use it to support "every perspective is right!" Teams across the organization must be able to access the data, understand it in context, and get that information out at a time when it can be of value. A visual representation of the curation of established perspectives, such as an "insight compass," supports immediate awareness for the viewer and represents to what extent the data have been cultivated. Also, comparisons to frameworks like the capability maturity model are an excellent guide for determining if established behaviors are advancing.

As much as visionaries hope for employees with limitless energy to drive the organization forward, the onus falls back on leadership to build an informed and intelligent culture that embraces diversity, different perspectives, and awareness of the larger context. Eliminate silos between departments and foster teamwork among them. A joint vision drives purpose, especially when individual activities directly relate to larger goals.

The road to an intelligent organization does not lie exclusively in predicting and managing what (might) happen next but in anticipating change. The coming Machineforce Age, where man and machine directly align, equals infinite possibilities for growth and development. An opportunity to give people a voice, foster innovation, and shape a more human-centered technological future. By using the principles outlined in this book while exploiting AI strategically, businesses can address today's challenges and set a strong foundation for the future— foundations that support humans with AI as a force multiplier.

Building an AI-Driven Culture

Driving organizational change, akin to dancing with continual grace and fluidity, is the new normal—a state to acknowledge, accept, and embrace as leaders. Where MTV Video Jockey's (VJs) endeavored to take us on musical road trips, leaders today need the flexibility of an All Terain Vechile (ATV), not knowing what twists or turns lie ahead. Organizational leadership must do more to engage and motivate teams, provide customized education, and bring everyone on the journey toward new ways of working. The fluxive leader embraces change as a learning opportunity, recognizing its mental challenges. They maintain composure and guide their team through uncharted territory, mitigating the potential for exhaustion.

Progress is more than statistics; it's visible organizational behavioral changes. Slight modifications in behavior are natural markers of further profound transformation, and the most crucial constant in the journey is to welcome new information and learn from it. As leaders on shifting sands, embracing a fluxive mindset helps value events taking place, new information, and continuous learning to drive the organization forward.

Fluxive leaders support organizational influence architecture—the detailed knowledge, monitoring, and manipulation of an organization's large and intricate influencing factors to support its capacity for innovation and adaptability. They recognize patterns and create narratives to understand the underlying motivations of both internal and external audiences. Fluxive leaders embrace the power of influence to foster a culture of adaptability and innovation.

Building an AI-driven culture is essential for continuous learning, adaptability, and innovation. It empowers individuals and organizations to thrive in the face of technological advancements and stay ahead of the competition. Fluxive leadership is crucial in this context, as leaders must be willing to adapt behaviors to embrace new technologies and foster a culture of lifelong learning. By embracing AI-driven systems and promoting a mindset of adaptability and innovation, fluxive leaders can create a workforce that is agile, resilient, and ready to meet future challenges.

Evolving Beyond Insights

Insights and contextual understanding fuel action. Data can contain a treasure trove of insights, but data are only as valuable as the actions they inform and the changes they help create. Nowadays, we can go beyond observing and idea generation, with data helping to provide extended details to the organizational roadmap. Data input serves as raw material that generates insights, and people create interpretations out of it, resulting in practical strategies. We can uncover those growth gems by tackling problems in real time, implementing findings, and busting the status quo of static reports. Here are vital strategies whereby organizations can develop a culture that does something and allows others to do it:

Strategically Invest in Technology

- Pick the right tools: Pick technology solutions that meet your organizational requirements and long-term vision. Focus on scale and stature.
- Build a tactical toolbox: Create guidelines and document standard tool usage to ensure team consistency and efficiency. Every member should know and adopt what's in the tactical toolbox instead of having one-off use cases for a particular technology. It's not necessarily "if" a platform can support needs but "how" it can, which brings us back to the need for cross-organizational alignment.

Empower Your Technical Team

- Break the silos: Get your tech team involved in strategic thinking and business initiatives.
- Promote cross-team and cross-training: Ensure that teams understand each other's goals and how technology can help them achieve them.

Build a Culture of Experimentation

- Create a safe environment: Allow employees to be innovative, question the prevailing culture, and test new technologies without fear of failure.
- Drive collaboration across silos: Draw upon different viewpoints to yield fresh ideas and outputs.
- Knowledge sharing: Promote transparency and knowledge dispensation for everyone's collective growth.

Communicate Effectively

- Customize communication: Change how you communicate to match how different audiences interpret messages. Avoid technical language, keep things simple for broad audiences, and hone in on specific teams' messages.

AI adoption is not a one-size-fits-all endeavor. Organizations must recognize the nuances of their unique needs and tailor strategies accordingly. This will likely involve demonstrating the cost-benefit analysis of AI, highlighting the potential to save money, enhance competitive advantage, or improve experiences. Trust and credibility are built through transparency and a focus on using AI for positive outcomes rather than solely for profit or competitive gain.

AI is undoubtedly a force in and of itself; it can give us marvels and, to some extent, may mislead human will to a dangerous path. Great innovation is balanced with the conscious instinct of ethics, but always just for societal good. For each organization, it's an opportunity to rewrite the narrative of AI so that it does not just serve as a tool for business profit maximization but contributes to uplifting society.

Fostering a culture of sharing, accountability, and responsible AI development can strengthen interaction frameworks and determine how modern tools should operate to assist humanity. Organizations can lead by example, creating extended ecosystems for harmonious interactions. By encouraging collaboration, promoting transparency, and holding ourselves accountable for the ethical use of AI, we can ensure that these powerful technologies are used for all benefit.

Sustaining Energy: The Never-Ending Journey

In 2014, I had the privilege of running my first marathon with a dear friend. I can't help but find it an insightful synonym for the journey ahead for many organizations. Anticipating the event, you can practice, evaluate the course, and plan for the best outcomes. When the day comes, the gun signals that it's time to move forward. Regardless of the differences in everyone's skills and preparation, the race is on, and it's time to take your first step. I noticed, for everyone, that regardless of skill, training, equipment, and physical condition, there's a pivotal cadence to embody:

Pace at your speed
Shorten your stride when the path is hard
Lengthen your stride when momentum carries you forward
Slow and stop, yes, stop, to rehydrate
Deal with problems along the way
Always remember the end state and
finish finish finish

Embrace the Journey

Often, in our journey of chasing goals, we focus on the destination and look to reach that finish line for acknowledgment—milestones. And yet, how often do we take a moment to ponder the trip: the side trips that led nowhere, the stops at rest areas along the interstate of life during which it seemed one illusion had been exchanged for another.

AI transformation is deeply embedded in the personal stories of individuals and organizations alike. It interrupts the status quo, pushes comfort limits, and requires us to be strong in our flexibility. Sound familiar? It echoes the profound goings-on that changes our lives. But how do we prepare for the journey and ensure our eyes are on the prize?

The solution is fluid leadership—accepting change and fostering psychological agility. It's about taking risks, failing, and learning your way through. Growth is not a straight line; it's an unending series of ups and downs. It brings comfort in the journey—what it teaches you and how much inevitable growth is involved. To master this changing environment, be guided by such principles as:

Look past the commandment: Push to add value in response.
Reimagine reinventing your workflows with the power of AI.
Discover diverse views: There are multiple ways to interpret data.
Enrich the view with various perspectives and an appreciation of history. If you need to experience this, attend the following local sporting event and watch the game from two different seats—it may be the same, but you'll see it very differently.
Focus on actionable intelligence: There is no reason to collect data when you can turn that information into quality decisions and impact actions.
Make friends with agony: Change is hard but keeps us alive.
Perspective is vital—consider setbacks as a course correction, an unplanned chance to adjust and improve.
Walk the talk: Be a case study for fluxive leadership. In life, be fluid and adapt, fail forward fast, and use positive reinforcement.

Following these mindset guides can help you on your journey to an AI transformation that will arm the knowledge, strength, and grit needed for evolution. After all, it is about making it to the end and what that path could change in us. Drive the human spirit to innovate and prepare for what is possible with AI in a way not seen before. It's more than adopting new technology; it is about unleashing our best selves in a manner that humans and AI come together to create a more fantastic version of things. Set a path in the AI era as the disappointment period, building a foundation for your exponential organization in the Machineforce Era.

References

1. McKinsey & Company. 2024. "The State of AI in Early 2024: Gen AI Adoption Spikes and Starts to Generate Value," May 30. www.mckinsey. com/capabilities/quantumblack/our-insights/the-state-of-ai.

2. Thaler, R.H., and C.R. Sunstein. 2008. *Nudge: Improving Decisions About Health, Wealth, and Happiness*. New Haven: Yale University Press.

3. Catalyser. 2023. "The Role of Companies on Social Issues," July 11. https:// catalyser.com/blog/social-impact/the-role-of-companies-on-social-issues.

4. Resnik D.B., and K.C. Elliott. 2016. "The Ethical Challenges of Socially Responsible Science." *Accountability in Research* 23 (1): 31–46. doi: 10.1080/08989621.2014.1002608. PMID: 26193168; PMCID: PMC4631672.

5. Smith, A. 2010. *The Theory of Moral Sentiments*. National Geographic Books.

6. "Amazon's Monopoly—Institute for Local Self-Reliance." 2024. *Institute for Local Self-Reliance*, May 13. https://ilsr.org/articles/amazons-monopoly/.

7. Doerr, J. 2018. *Measure What Matters: OKRs—The Simple Idea That Drives 10x Growth*. Portfolio Penguin.

8. Heaven, W.D. 2020. "Our Weird Behavior During the Pandemic Is Messing With AI Models." *MIT Technology Review*, December 10. www.technology review.com/2020/05/11/1001563/covid-pandemic-broken-ai-machine-learning-amazon-retail-fraud-humans-in-the-loop/.

9. DataRobot. 2024. "DataRobot Opens Up Its Platform for COVID-19 Response Efforts," July 30. www.datarobot.com/newsroom/press/ datarobot-opens-up-its-platform-for-covid-19-response-efforts/.

10. Aite-Novarica. n.d. "COVID-19 Has Broken Your Predictive Models." https://aite-novarica.com/blogs/eric-weisburg/covid-19-has-broken-your-predictive-models.

11. Pieter, and Pieter. 2024. "The Four Levels of Data Maturity That You Should Know About." *COMPUTD*, March 21. https://computd. nl/4-levels-of-data-maturity/.

12. Harford, T. 2012. *Adapt: Why Success Always Starts With Failure*. Picador.

13. "Data Science Is a Team Sport." n.d. *JMP*. www.jmp.com/en_us/articles/data-science-is-a-team-sport.html.

14. Gallup, Inc. 2023. "From Appreciation to Equity: How Recognition Reinforces DEI in the Workplace." https://assets.ctfassets.net/hff6luki1ys4/4lom3PUaKYOIaDbZaMsujC/57eb225b758c5aa2dcf82f4dd1a6c842/from-appreciation-to-equity.pdf.

15. Liao, G., J. Zhou, and J. Yin. April 2022. "Effect of Organizational Socialization of New Employees on Team Innovation Performance: A Cross-Level Model." Psychology Research and Behavior Management 21 (15):1017–1031. doi: 10.2147/PRBM.S359773. PMID: 35480713; PMCID: PMC9037896.

16. Gartner & Thomas McCall. 2018. "Gartner Survey Shows Organizations Are Slow to Advance in Data and Analytics," February 5. www.gartner.com/en/newsroom/press-releases/2018-02-05-gartner-survey-shows-organizations-are-slow-to-advance-in-data-and-analytics.

17. Olavsrud, T. 2024. "Ten Famous AI Disasters." CIO, April 17. www.cio.com/article/190888/5-famous-analytics-and-ai-disasters.html.

18. Bishop, G.J. 2021. *Unf*ck Yourself: Get Out of Your Head and Into Your Life.* Yellow Kite.

19. Markova, D., and A. McArthur. 2015. *Collaborative Intelligence: Thinking With People Who Think Differently*. Random House.

20. Chrissis, M.B., M. Konrad, and S. Shrum. 2011. "CMMI for Development: Guidelines for Process Integration and Product Improvement." *Addison-Wesley Professional*.

21. Geiger, C. 2016. "Run That Pizza Through the Test Kitchen." Hoards.com, October 10. https://hoards.com/article-19477-run-that-pizza-through-the-test-kitchen.html.

22. Cialdini, R.B., PhD. 1993. *Influence (rev): The Psychology of Persuasion*. Harper Collins.

23. Konstantinovic, D. 2022b. "How 'Services' Became Apple's Fastest-Growing Revenue Category." *EMARKETER*, May 3. www.emarketer.com/content/how-services-became-apple-s-fastest-growing-revenue-category.

24. Thomke, S. March–April 2020. "Building a Culture of Experimentation." *Harvard Business Review* 98 (2): 40–48.

25. KPMG. n.d. "Generative AI Has an Increasing Effect on the Workforce and Productivity—KPMG Survey." https://kpmg.com/us/en/media/news/kpmg-genai-workforce-survey.html.

26. Ikenberry, G.J., and J.S. Nye. 2004. "Soft Power: The Means to Success in World Politics." *Foreign Affairs* 83 (3): 136. https://doi.org/10.2307/20033985.

27. Scientific American. 2024. "Forget Survival of the Fittest: It Is Kindness That Counts," February 20. www.scientificamerican.com/article/kindness-emotions-psychology/.

28. Berger, J. 2016. *Invisible Influence: The Hidden Forces That Shape Behavior*, 59. Simon & Schuster.

29. Iansiti, M., and K.R. Lakhani. 2020. *Competing in the Age of AI: Strategy and Leadership When Algorithms and Networks Run the World*, XV. Harvard Business Press.

About the Illustrator

Adam Sollien, a passionate artist hailing from the picturesque landscapes of Upstate New York, honed his creative talents at the Sage College of Albany, where he earned a degree in Illustration. Since graduating, Adam has immersed himself in the vibrant local art scene, lending his artistic vision to various projects. He's become a sought-after collaborator, crafting distinctive logos and eye-catching mixed-media designs that capture the essence of local businesses and the energy of sporting events. His work is a testament to his dedication to his craft and his love for the region that inspires him.

About the Author

Sean W. Smith, a seasoned expert with over two decades of experience in data and advanced analytics, is a recognized thought leader at the forefront of data science, artificial intelligence, and organizational transformation. His career is dedicated to harnessing the power of technology to drive impactful business outcomes while laying the groundwork for a positive and collaborative future with AI.

As a strategic leader and tactical manager, Sean heads customer success teams for next-generation AI products, guiding seasoned industry and technical professionals. His fluxive leadership style, rooted in adaptability and a focus on performance, fosters individual growth and long-term organizational success. He champions building solid foundations for a future where humans and machines work together seamlessly.

Sean's passion extends beyond his professional role. He actively participates in events, panels, and focus groups related to data, analytics, and AI, contributing to the industry's knowledge base and fostering community.

An unwavering believer in the transformative potential of data and AI, Sean inspires others to embrace these technologies and the boundless possibilities they offer. Through his work and engagements, he instills optimism and excitement about the industry's future, emphasizing the importance of building a positive symbiotic machineforce.

Index

www.ingramcontent.com/pod-product-compliance
Lightning Source LLC
Chambersburg PA
CBHW061304220326
41599CB00026B/4725